NOT the MET

NOT the MET

Exploring the Smaller Museums of Manhattan

By Janel Halpern
& Harvey Appelbaum

PELICAN PUBLISHING COMPANY
Gretna 2013

*The word "Pelican" and the depiction of a pelican are
trademarks of Pelican Publishing Company, Inc., and are
registered in the U.S. Patent and Trademark Office.*

Library of Congress Cataloging-in-Publication Data

Halpern, Janel.
  Not the Met : exploring the smaller museums of Manhattan / by Janel
Halpern and Harvey Appelbaum.
    pages cm
  Includes index.
  ISBN 978-1-4556-1868-2 (pbk. : alk. paper) — ISBN 978-1-4556-1869-9
(e-book) 1. Museums—New York (State)—New York—Guidebooks.
2. Manhattan (New York, N.Y.)—Guidebooks. 3. New York (N.Y.)—
Guidebooks. I. Appelbaum, Harvey. II. Title.
  AM13.N5H35 2013
  069.025747'1—dc23
                                                          2013016321

Printed in Korea

Published by Pelican Publishing Company, Inc.
1000 Burmaster Street, Gretna, Louisiana 70053

To our families, who were supportive and patient during the two-plus years during which we visited all the museums we describe in this book. To the museum executives who applauded our work and urged us to continue it. To all those worldwide who love museums as we do.

Geographical Index

East Side above 42nd Street

Asia Society—New York
Austrian Cultural Forum New York
Caribbean Cultural Center African Diaspora Institute
China Institute Gallery
Cooper-Hewitt, National Design Museum
The Czech Center New York
El Museo del Barrio New York
French Institute/Alliance Française
The Frick Collection
German Consulate New York
The Grolier Club
Herbert and Eileen Bernard Museum of Judaica
The Institute for the Study of the Ancient World
Instituto Cervantes
The Japan Society
The Jewish Museum
Korean Cultural Service
Kosciuszko Foundation
Mount Vernon Hotel Museum and Garden
The Museum of American Illustration
The Museum of Comic and Cartoon Art
Museum of the City of New York
National Academy Museum
The National Jazz Museum in Harlem
Neue Galerie
Onassis Cultural Center

East Side below 42nd Street

American Numismatic Society and the Federal Reserve Bank of New York
Anthology Film Archives
Fraunces Tavern Museum
The Gabarron Foundation: Carriage House Center for the Arts
Grey Art Gallery
Italian American Museum
Merchant's House Museum

The Morgan Library and Museum
Museum at Eldridge Street
Museum of Chinese in America
Museum of Sex
New Museum
The New York City Police Museum
Salmagundi Art Club
Scandinavia House
The Tenement Museum
Theodore Roosevelt Birthplace
The Ukrainian Museum

West Side above 42nd Street

American Folk Art Museum
Bard Graduate Center: Decorative Arts, Design History, Material Culture
Children's Museum of Manhattan
Dyckman Farmhouse Museum
The Hamilton Grange National Memorial
The Hispanic Society of America
International Center of Photography
Morris-Jumel Mansion
Museum of Arts and Design
Museum of Biblical Art
New-York Historical Society Museum and Library
The Paley Center for Media
Rose Museum at Carnegie Hall
The Schomburg Center for Research in Black Culture
The Studio Museum in Harlem

West Side below 42nd Street

The Anne Frank Center USA
Center for Architecture
The Center for Book Arts
Center for Jewish History
Children's Museum of the Arts
The Drawing Center
The Forbes Galleries
The Hebrew Union College-Jewish Institute of Religion Museum—
    New York

Preface

Not the Met: Exploring the Smaller Museums of Manhattan is a book for people who love museums. The idea for this book took shape when we saw a long list of New York City museums published by the New York City Department of Cultural Affairs. Though we are both life-long residents of the city, we had not visited most of the museums on the list—nor had we even heard of a good many. This came as a surprise, and so we decided to do something about it. Out of our weekly expeditions visiting the smaller museums of Manhattan came this book.

We both love the Metropolitan Museum of Art (the Met) and have visited its glories countless times. So, probably, have you. Its familiar name in our title is not meant as a slight to this great museum. We are attempting only to underscore our notion that you already know the Met and, like us, have visited it perhaps several times. Also most likely familiar to you are the Museum of Modern Art, the Guggenheim, the American Museum of Natural History, and the Whitney Museum of American Art. However, we are also aware that you probably have not visited many of the "smaller" museums that we cover in this volume—and we are absolutely sure that those experiences are bound to be wonderful. Perhaps you, too, are ready for a new and stimulating experience. During our years of visits, we have been astonished repeatedly by the museums we have encountered, particularly those about which we formerly knew nothing. We want you to know about them, too.

Some people have asked us about what constitutes a smaller museum. Our immediate response to that question is, "Not the square footage." Some of the museums we write about and photograph are quite large. For example, the Morgan Library and Museum and the Museum of the City of New York both originated in buildings once used as private homes. The newly renovated New-York Historical Society Museum and Library is almost a full city block square. However, none of these exemplary museums can compete with the size of the Met, the breadth of its incredible holdings, or the numbers of its visitors. What distinguishes most of these smaller museums of Manhattan is that they are not as well known and they provide a unique look at all of New York's cultures and influences.

We want to caution you that most museums change their exhibits from two to four times a year, so the likelihood that you will see exactly what we saw is exceedingly small. We suggest that you contact the museum to learn whether its visiting hours have changed and to learn about its current exhibit. However, we hope that our descriptions and photos will give you a taste of the flavor or essence of the museums and encourage you to see these wonderful institutions for yourself. Most of our photographs are original, but some have been donated by the museums themselves. Last but not least, have a great time museum going!

Janel Halpern and Harvey Appelbaum

NOT the
MET

American Folk Art Museum

Location and Transit

2 Lincoln Square
(212) 595-9533
folkartmuseum.org
Subway: 1
Bus: M5, M7, M11, M20, M66,
M104

Hours and Admission

Tues.-Sat.	**12-7:30 p.m.**
Sun.	**12-6:00 p.m.**
Mon.	**Closed**
Free	

Our visit to the American Folk Art Museum was both exciting and somewhat sad. The museum has relocated to its original home on Columbus Avenue across from Lincoln Center after a ten-year stay in a marvelous building next door to the Museum of Modern Art on East 53rd Street. However, it fortunately has retained the exhaustive collection of folk art for which it is known. This fact, along with the exhibit we saw, did a great deal to assuage the loss of the former structure.

On the walls of its one-floor exhibit space, the American Folk Art Museum displayed a series of spectacular quilts. At the entry area of the museum, a visitor was astounded and moved by an enormous hanging marking the events of September 11, 2001. There on the wall, on a quilt stitched by many hands, were images created from many colored cotton patches of the two buildings, the firefighters and police who rushed to the scene, and the names of those lost on that terrible day.

The rest of the exhibition formed a more uplifting experience. An alcove held "show quilts" that had one image in common: stars. This was a popular theme in the late nineteenth century, when they were created. One small starburst crib quilt bore a star in its center with yellow and brown stars around it stitched onto an orange background. The *All American Star Quilt*, created between 1940 and 1945, bore red and blue stars on white. The red stars contained blue stars. This quilt reflected the great patriotism during World War II. *Le Moyne Star Variation Quilt* entertained the eye with brightly colored red, yellow, blue, green, and floral stars, made by Lucinda Toomer in 1981. The Le Moyne Star, formed by eight equilateral diamond shapes, is said to be the oldest star pattern. It came into American quilt making in the last quarter of the eighteenth century.

The museum holds a panoply of star quilts, since in the United States, many artisans included these symbols in their work due to their religious connotations. Some of these uses were quite unusual. A mariner's compass quilt, which centered around a four pointed star, was obviously made for the use of a sea-going man. The *Stars over Hawaii Quilt*, stitched by Mary K. Borkowski in 1979, was green on a yellow and white background. The yellow star in the center was surrounded by four large green leaves with fish emerging from them. It is a splendid reminder of the beautiful state that it symbolizes.

The museum in its current configuration has easily accessible bathrooms but no eating area. However, there are many restaurants in this part of town. In addition, if one takes a short walk across Broadway and down to Columbus Circle, a hungry visitor will find a large Whole Foods Market that has a seating area and lots to choose from.

American Numismatic Society and the Federal Reserve Bank of New York

Location and Transit—American Numismatic Society

75 Varick Street
(212) 571-4470
numismatics.org
Subway: 1, A, C, E
Bus: M1, M6, M20

Location and Transit—Federal Reserve Bank

44 Maiden Lane
(212) 720-5000
newyorkfed.org
Subway: 2, 3, 4, 5, A, C, J, Z
Bus: M9, M15, M103

Hours and Admission

Mon.-Fri.	9:30 a.m.-4:30 p.m.
Sat.-Sun.	Closed
General admission	$10
Members and students with ID	Free

Hours and Admission

Mon.-Fri.	10 a.m.-3 p.m., except bank holidays
Sat.-Sun.	Closed
	Online reservations only
	Free

If you are interested in money—and really, who isn't?—a trip to the American Numismatic Society is just what you might enjoy. A membership organization, the American Numismatic Society occupies two locations. The society has a membership of more than two thousand coin collectors, coin dealers, artists, sculptors, and scholars. Its main offices are at Varick

Street in lower Manhattan, where it houses the largest collection of volumes and other publications about money in the United States, including rare books on the subject, and also offers a small exhibit space in the entry hall. When we visited, we saw an interesting presentation about Victor David Brenner, an artist and sculptor who designed the Lincoln penny. This building is any numismatic researcher's heaven.

The society's main exhibitions are held in the Federal Reserve Bank of New York, which deserves several hours of its own for the full experience. We hurried further downtown to see two wonderful exhibits, *Drachmas, Doubloons, and Dollars: The History of Money* and *Funny Money: The Fight of the United States Secret Service against Counterfeit Money*.

At *Drachmas, Doubloons, and Dollars*, we saw the varied forms of money used by man throughout history, including coins, shells, salt, tokens, beads, gold, paper money, and credit cards. The coins and paper money were works of art—sometimes jewelry—and also occasionally served as political messages. Thus, in looking at them, we learned a good deal about the societies to which they belonged. The exhibit included more than eight hundred pieces from the society's collection, including a Brasher doubloon, an 1804 dollar, and a Confederate half dollar. We also saw the world's most valuable coin, a 1933 Double Eagle twenty-dollar coin.

Funny Money was actually quite serious. This exhibit displayed forged notes from around the world. We also saw photographs of counterfeiting operations as well as the varied ingenious methods counterfeiters use to smuggle their wares into the United States. In order to foil these criminals, authorities who issue money create design elements that are more and more difficult to emulate, such as watermarks, security threads, color-shifting ink, special paper, signatures, the US seal, and unique numbering. We also learned that most counterfeit US money is created abroad.

A few hours in this museum will augment your interest in the paper or coins in your wallet.

The Anne Frank Center USA

Location and Transit

44 Park Place
(212) 431-7993
annefrank.com
Subway: 2, 3, 4, 5, A, C, E, N
Bus: M5, M9, M22, M103

Hours and Admission

Tues.-Sat.	**10 a.m.-5 p.m.**
Sun.-Mon. and holidays	**Closed**
Adults	**$8**
Seniors and students	**$5**
Children 7 and under	**Free**

We were among the lucky first visitors to the newly relocated and renovated Anne Frank Center USA. It is a very small museum that makes a very big impact on its guests. Who would have guessed that there was a museum honoring the legacy of Anne Frank right here in New York City? What one sees at the entrance of the new Park Place storefront museum sets the theme of the Anne Frank Center. In Anne's own words, "How lovely to think that no one need wait a moment, we can start slowly changing the world! How lovely that everyone, great and small, can make their contribution to introducing justice straightaway."

In the entry to the museum, there is a wooden model of the house and secret attic where Anne Frank lived. Another such model resides at the Anne Frank House in Amsterdam. Two large black and white photographs cover the walls to document the raid on May 26, 1943, that marked the ultimate demise of this now-famous young German-Jewish girl, carried out by the Henneicke Column, Dutch bounty hunters who tracked down eight thousand Jews and earned 7.50 guilders for every Jew—a 1940s value of $3.00 per person. The captured Jews were sent to transit camp Westerbrook, and then deported to concentration camps. It was at the Bergen-Belsen camp that Anne died at the age of fifteen. It is this kind of injustice that the Anne Frank Center was established to fight.

The major museum exhibit is a free-standing curved room with one wall bearing a color photograph of the inside of the Secret Annex, where the Frank family and others took refuge. This room also contains five iPads that give the visitors interactive information about the diary, the Secret Annex, growing up in hiding, the helpers, and being on the inside looking out. I found the material covering the helpers, which provided photographs of and interviews with an aging Miep Gies and other heroic people, particularly moving.

The Anne Frank Center also manages a traveling exhibit program, directs an education center on the lower floor for class visits, annually awards a college scholarship to a deserving high school student, and develops educational materials and training for teachers and students. On the walls of the education center were photographs of the Frank family before World War II.

There is no food service at the center but plenty of restaurants around it.

Anthology Film Archives

Location and Transit

32 2nd Avenue
(212) 505-5181
anthologyfilmarchives.org
Subway: 6, F
Bus: M15

Hours and Admission

Tickets available at the box office
  on the day of the show
General admission $10
Seniors, students, and children 12
  and under $8
Members $6

Anthology Film Archives can send a movie lover into rhapsodies. In its red-brick building—a former jail and courthouse on lower Second Avenue—one finds a treasure trove of cinema, from its origins through the present. Having opened its doors in 1970, Anthology Film Archives is dedicated to exploring avant-garde film as an art form and its film makers.

The Archives fulfills its mission through film preservation and screenings, library acquisitions and holdings, education through outreach, and awards. It has created a repertory named the Essential Cinema Collection, which includes works by Stan Brakhage, Jean Cocteau, Bruce Conner, Carl Dreyer, Maya Deren, Sergei Eisenstein, D. W. Griffith, and scores of other film makers, including well-known present-day film artists. In addition, many of the film stills, frame enlargements, audio records, and other documents have been digitally scanned and are now available on the Web site for public review.

Almost any evening of the week, a visitor can commandeer a comfortable seat in either the nine-hundred- or seventy-seat theater and see a film he or she could not see anywhere else. The day we visited, we might have seen Ken Russells's *Lisztomania* or *Color of Pomegranates* by Sergei Paradjanov, part of the Archives' Anti-Biopics film series of avant-garde biographies that seek to convey the reality and essence of a human life without the star-studded Hollywood formula for film biography.

Asia Society—New York

Location and Transit
725 Park Avenue
(212) 288-6400
asiasociety.org
Subway: 6, F
Bus: M1, M2, M3, M4, M30, M66, M101, M102

Hours and Admission

Tues.-Thurs., Sat.-Sun.	11 a.m.-6 p.m.
Fri.	11 a.m.-9 p.m.
Mon.	Closed
Adults	$10
Seniors	$7
Students with ID	$5
Members and children under 16	Free
Fri., 6-9 p.m.	Free

The Asia Society is the result of the Rockefeller interest in bringing the art and culture of the Far East to the United States. Its expansive entry hall with walls and ceilings of honey-colored wood and a floor of white tile affords an instant reminder of Japanese homes and spaces. The day we visited, square plexiglass columns held beautiful and rare Chinese bronze statues from the collection of Mr. and Mrs. John D. Rockefeller III. The appetizer of bronzes led to a fuller meal of exquisite pieces on the second floor.

The art at the Asia Society is generally on loan from organizations and individuals all over the world, so one can see something different every time one visits. When we were there, we saw Hanging Fire: Contemporary Art from Pakistan, which offered some monumental modern paintings and sculptures, most of which had a dramatic political bent, reflecting the societal turmoil that has roiled contemporary Pakistan. For example, one of the major painters in this exhibit, Zahoor ul Akhlaq, a man of great artistic stature, a teacher, and a mentor to many younger artists, had been assassinated because of his political works. Seeing this exhibit gave one a deeper understanding of the issues with which Pakistan and the Western World grapple.

The Asia Society has a wonderful main-floor restaurant, where one can lunch among live trees in a light-filled atrium. Many of the plants reach to the two-story ceiling. The museum has elevators to reach all of the galleries and a lovely shop. Because of its location on bustling Park Avenue, we recommend taking public transportation.

Austrian Cultural Forum New York

Location and Transit
11 East 52nd Street
(212) 319-5300
acfny.org
Subway: 6, B, D, E, F, M
Bus: M1, M2, M3, M4, M5

Hours and Admission

Mon.-Sat.	**10 a.m.-6 p.m.**
Sun.	**Closed**
Free	

The Austrian Cultural Forum is right across the street from the Olympic Towers and the Onassis Cultural Center. It is a unique, contemporary architectural delight that stands out among the other more mundane buildings on the same Midtown block. It is a green, glass-windowed building that narrows as it stretches upward and away from the street. Fondly called "the lighthouse," it is a beacon in the city, containing a concert hall, a literary center, a community space for Austrian artists and intellectuals trying to establish themselves in the USA, a department of the Austrian Foreign Ministry, and, of course an exhibition space.

We were somewhat mystified by *Serbia: Frequently Asked Questions*, the exhibit we saw. Presented under the auspices of the European Union National Institutes for Culture and in partnership with the Museum of Contemporary Art Belgrade, the works we saw by contemporary Serbian artists shared a critical stance toward processes of economic and political transition as well as the pain and turbulence of the war.

The artworks were all very individual. Zoran Todorović presented an entire room filled with strange looking mounds of unusual blankets made of three tons of human hair collected from hairdressers and military barracks. Stefanos Tsivopoulos provided a two-screen video—one screen showed the testimony of a Serbian soldier describing the atrocities of the Bosnian war, while an actor repeated the stories on the other screen—leaving it up to the viewers to decide which man is the real veteran. Vlatka Horvat presented her video *This Here and That There,* in which chairs in a shallow pond are continually rearranged as a metaphor for dealing with the loss of geographic roots and social communities. Anri Sala presented a video, *Natural Mystic,* in which a man from Belgrade uses his vocal chords to flawlessly imitate the sound of a Tomahawk missile, a common noise heard in Belgrade during the NATO bombing campaign over Serbia in 1999.

As we studied the artworks, their purpose became clearer to us as a way to understand how the war in Bosnia changed Serbia and Serbian artists—probably forever.

Bard Graduate Center: Decorative Arts, Design History, Material Culture

Location and Transit

18 West 86th Street
(212) 501-3023
bgc.bard.edu
Subway: 1, B, C
Bus: M7, M10, M11, M86

Hours and Admission

Tues.-Wed., Fri.-Sun.	11 a.m.-5 p.m.
Thurs.	11 a.m.-8 p.m.
Mon.	Closed
General admission	$7
Seniors and students with ID	$5
Thurs. 5-8 p.m.	Free

For those who are interested in the decorative arts or interior design, a couple hours at the Bard Graduate Center Gallery might be a better-spent afternoon than picking up the latest home magazine. First of all, it will cost you very little, and second, it will be enlightening. BGC is a division of Bard College, established for students studying for their MAs or PhDs in the decorative arts. Bard College owns three buildings on the block, used as classrooms, a library, lecture halls, and administrative offices. BGC, established in 1993, mounts two large and two small exhibitions each year in its associated gallery.

We saw the exhibit *Knoll Textiles, 1945-2010*, which provided an extensive view of the textile division of Knoll Furniture, its products, and the major designers. The Knoll Textile Division was established by Hans and Florence Knoll in 1947, one year after their marriage. Hans had established the furniture company in 1940, and Florence Schust had joined the firm to help create the planning division responsible for interior design. They believed that the textiles that covered their furniture should advance the modern sensibility of the furniture itself, and they favored innovative texture and color. Florence herself was responsible for some of the earliest designs, but some fifty designers were involved during the years covered in the exhibit. In 1978, the Knolls added wallpaper design, began to employ Japanese designers, and explored creating fabrics out of plastic. In a real sense, the company was responsible for the trends in modern fabric design.

What we saw was exciting, beginning with the first floor—large screen-printed swatches or coverings on real furniture reminded us of early modern design. These fabrics used geometric figures, squares, circles, and triangles in deep colors. We were envious of the freshness and daring of the fabrics and wall coverings—a sign of a well-conceived and well-executed show.

Courtesy Bard Graduate Center

rtesy Bard Graduate Center   *Courtesy Bard Graduate Center*

Caribbean Cultural Center African Diaspora Institute

Location and Transit

120 East 125th Street
(212) 307-7420
cccadi.org
Subway: 2, 3
Bus: M11, M15, M60, M101

Hours and Admission

Mon.-Fri.	10 a.m.-6 p.m.
Sat.-Sun.	Closed
Free	

Previously located across from the Time Warner Center, the Caribbean Cultural Center African Diaspora Institute (CCCADI) moved to Harlem into a decommissioned historic landmark firehouse. The bright and vivid colors of the Caribbean on the outside of the building invited visitors to look inside at the gift shop and then lured them upstairs to the gallery.

When we were there, the CCADI was in the midst of a celebration of New Orleans culture called *Saving Our Soul: From the Big Easy to the Big Apple.* As part of this cultural and intellectual festival, the institute presented *S.O.S.: Magic, Revelry, and Resistance in Post-Katrina New Orleans Art*, which featured the colorful work of young New Orleans artists, including Lorna Williams, J'Renee, Bruce Davenport, Abdul Aziz, Terrence Sanders, and Ayo Y. Scott. These artists displayed works that reflected their deep emotional responses to Hurricane Katrina and the political debacle that accompanied it. The mediums included large mixed-media collage, voodoo dolls, and several unflattering depictions of then-president George W. Bush, particularly a large portrait in which he resembled the Joker of *Batman* fame.

The CCCADI also schedules regular lectures and concerts, usually related to its main mission of celebrating Caribbean and African culture.

Center for Architecture

Location and Transit

536 LaGuardia Place
(212) 683-0023
cfa.aiany.org
Subway: 6, A, B, C, D, E, F, M, N, R
Bus: M1, M15, M20

Hours and Admission

Mon.-Fri.	**9 a.m.-8 p.m.**
Sat.	**11 a.m.-5 p.m.**
Sun.	**Closed**
Free	

A beautiful Sukkah (a Jewish three-sided religious structure made of natural materials) made of twigs graced the large window at the Center for Architecture and drew visitors into the main exhibit space. The Sukkah was one of the winning structures of the Sukkah City competition in 2010. The center is home to the New York chapter of the American Institute of Architects (AIA) and the Center for Architecture Foundation. Its goal is to improve the quality and sustainability of the built environment; foster exchange between the design, construction, and real estate communities; and encourage collaborations among these entities in New York and across the world.

It provides galleries on three floors, but the day we visited, the main and second floor galleries were being prepared for the next major exhibition. Thus, we were limited to an exhibit on the lower level called *NPNY2010*

(New Practices New York 2010). Included in this interesting exhibit were the seven winners of the biennial juried competition established by the New Practices Committee of the AIA New York chapter. All of the winners, young design or architectural firms, provided fascinating samples of their design ethos, which were all unusual and innovative. Each winner provided a large, loose-leaf booklet describing the projects in detail to accompany the miniature models, so that even a non-savvy visitor could appreciate the ideas and technical skill that went into each design. The exhibit also offered a special publication that further defined the ideas of the winners both through text and photograph.

One doesn't have to be an architect to belong to AIA. While many of its activities are for its professional members, many events are scheduled for the public at large. In fact, it holds public events four or five nights each week. The center provides a lecture hall, a library, and a training center, in addition to the roughly six exhibitions per year.

The center has an elevator but does not have a shop or a restaurant. Its location, in the heart of Greenwich Village, provides ample choice of marvelous eating places and interesting shopping.

The Center for Book Arts

Location and Transit

28 West 27th Street, 3rd Floor
(212) 481-0295
centerforbookarts.org
Subway: 1, 2, 3, 6, 7, B, D, F, N,
 Q, R
Bus: M1, M2, M3, M5, M6, M7,
 M10, M23, M34

Hours and Admission

Mon.-Fri.	**10 a.m.-6 p.m.**
Sat.	**10 a.m.-4 p.m.**
Sun.	**Closed**
Free	

Everyone reads a book now and then, and some read all of the time. Whether you are a casual reader or an absolute bookworm, you don't avoid them entirely—and anyway, you are reading a book right now! Have you ever wondered how a book is really made, how it morphs from a writer's manuscript into a bound object? Well, the Center for Book Arts is worth your visit.

The Center for Book Arts, the first such institution in the United States, has been providing opportunities to learn about fine book-making to book artists and visitors since 1974. It also offers courses in the printing arts as well as programs and readings for the general public. One section of the center is dedicated to the book-binding process.

At the center, you will get to see the steps that constitute book making with the guidance of a friendly and knowledgeable volunteer. In the printing section are three presses, surrounded by drawers full of wood and metal type. When we were there, two men were at the presses, one a member of the center, the other one of the five artists in residence. Both were intent upon laying the type for the books they were making. Warning us not to go too near the presses for fear that ink would find our clothing, our guide opened drawer after drawer of type, all different kinds and all possible sizes. Many of the typefaces we saw have made their way into our computers. Most are named for the printer who first created them.

The center's small, central gallery featured the work of innovative book artists. Here we saw Roger Rowley's humorous *Fruit Salad*, a panel of 72 8" x 9" inkjet prints showing different fruit salads Rowley made for his children. On another wall was Aspen Mays's *Every Leaf on a Tree*, 225 inkjet prints of every individual leaf of one tree. In this area also was Claude Closky's *Three Thousand Four Hundred and Fifteen Friday the 13ths*, a book filled with the dates of various Friday the 13ths. *My Things*, a book by Gabriela Gründler, held pictures of everything the artist owned.

Places to eat lunch or dinner abound in this neighborhood of New York City but not inside the center.

Center for Jewish History

Location and Transit
15 West 16th Street
(212) 294-8301
cjh.org
Subway: 1, 2, 3, 4, 5, 6, F, L, N, Q,
  R, V, W
Bus: M1, M2, M3, M5, M6, M7,
  M14, M23

Hours and Admission

Mon., Wed.	**9:30 a.m.-8 p.m.**
Tues., Thurs.	**9:30 a.m.-5 p.m.**
Fri.	**9:30 a.m.-3 p.m.**
Sun.	**11 a.m.-5 p.m.**
Sat.	**Closed**
Free	

We knew that the Center for Jewish History was a partnership of five organizations, but we did not know about the riches that awaited us inside the building. Affiliated with the Smithsonian, the center contains the collections of the American Jewish Historical Society, which documents the contributions of the Jewish community to American life; the American Sephardi Federation, which celebrates the wealth of the Sephardic heritage from around the world; the Leo Baeck Institute, which is devoted to the study and preservation of the legacy of German-speaking Jewry; Yeshiva University Museum, which showcases Jewish art, history, and culture through a variety of exhibitions and educational programs; and the YIVO Institute for Jewish Research, which is dedicated to the study and documentation of the history and culture of Ashkenazi Jews. The center includes the Ackman and Ziff Family Genealogy Institute and a state-of-the-art research library, holding a rare book room that contains the US Army Talmud.

Where to start in this treasure trove of Jewish history and culture? Our wonderful guide took us first to the Great Hall, which had originally been an outdoor courtyard between the buildings on Sixteenth and Seventeenth Streets. The hall itself was a work of art. It contained a remarkable floor by sculptor Michele Oka Doner called *Biblical Species,* which illustrated the seven species of plants—grapes, pomegranates, figs, wheat, barley, olives, and dates—that Moses's scouts brought back from their trip into the Promised Land to prove its bounty, inlaid in bronze and aluminum on greenish-black marble. The other art that dominates this space was

Luminous Manuscript by Diane Samuels, an entire wall installation that contained 80,500 pieces of glass, which cover 440 stone tiles that bear 112,640 alphabet characters from 57 writing systems. In addition, 34,500 glass tiles are inscribed with either numbers taken from archival documents or children's handprints. A nearby computer monitor aids visitors in identifying the various parts of the wall.

Each partner organization has its own exhibit space, and there was almost too much to properly recount. *Words and Memories* featured letters by Jewish soldiers and their families during World War II. *Painting to Remember,* presented by the Leo Baeck Institute, featured paintings of some of the destroyed synagogues of Germany as they had once been. It also included photos of the remains of synagogues destroyed during Kristallnacht.

A Journey through Jewish Worlds contained highlights from the Braginsky collection of Hebrew manuscripts. Braginsky, a Swiss banker and financier, has had a lifelong fascination with early illustrated manuscripts, a third of which were on loan. Breathtakingly illustrated Ketubahs, Haggadahs, and other books of Jewish rituals were on display. We saw the very modern paper assemblages by Andi Aronovitz, including the multi-colored paper *Vest of Prayers.*

The Palm Cafe, adjacent to the great hall, provides seating and vending machines but does not sell food.

Children's Museum of Manhattan

Location and Transit

212 West 83rd Street
(212) 721-1234
cmom.org
Subway: 1, 2, 3, A, B, C, D
Bus: M7, M10, M11, M79, M86,
**   M104**

Hours and Admission

Tues.-Sun.	**10 a.m.-5 p.m.**
Sat.	**10 a.m.-7 p.m.**
Mon.	**Closed**
Children and adults	**$11**
Seniors	**$7**
Members and children 12 months	
** and under**	**Free**

Sadly, adults must be accompanied by a child in order to visit the wonderland that is the Children's Museum of Manhattan. This rule is good protection from the hordes of unaccompanied adults who might otherwise go to the museum on their own and unwittingly push all the children out. In any case, it is a wonderful place for children and adults who have retained their sense of play.

All of the museum spaces are painted in exciting primary colors, and most of the rooms encourage active participation. One colorful wall decorated with a bare tree asked young participants to make their own poetry by placing word-filled leaves on the branches in whatever way they wished. One room, called Baby Babble, was dedicated to the very youngest visitors.

The secret of this museum is that all of its rooms and displays hide lessons inside all the fun. A room called the Little West Side, a fanciful replica of the area of the city in which the museum makes its home, is a place in which children can drive in a sit-in mail truck, buy and pay for groceries in a grocery store, play with an abacus made of small wooden animals in the pet shop, work an oversized clock, and sit in a New York City bus. While we were there, two children were giggling while mailing packages and whatever else they could put their hands on. This little boy and girl did not realize that they were learning language, math, and social skills at the same time.

On one wall in the hallway was a red, white, and blue quilt made up of quotes from children. "We are many colors, shapes, and sizes" read a patch sewn in by Marika Bailey of New York City. The quilt celebrates American holidays and inspires civic responsibility in its young viewers.

PlayWorks™, a very large space, was almost mayhem. Scores of children engaged in early-learning activities, using activity disks to make up stories and manning a fire engine to extinguish make-believe flames. Diego's World involved children in a series of animal rescue and care activities, which also taught scientific facts about animals, instilled a respect for the environment, created a desire to help others, and encouraged eagerness to learn more about the world.

The lowest level of the museum is designed for older children. Its displays included simplified scientific concepts such as circuits. These more complex displays allowed children to interact with the concepts by pushing, pulling, pounding, and doing anything else required to make the machine work, teaching a hands-on lesson along the way.

If parents can handle the noise, the Children's Museum of Manhattan is a great place to spend a few hours watching their children be happy and engaged.

Children's Museum of the Arts

Location and Transit

103 Charlton Street
(212) 274-0986
cmany.org
Subway: 1, A, B, C, D, E, F, M
Bus: M20, M21

Hours and Admission

Mon., Wed.	12-5 p.m.
Thurs.-Fri.	12-6 p.m.
Sat.-Sun.	10-5 p.m.
Tues.	Closed
General admission	$11
Members, seniors, and infants 12 mos. and under	Free
Thurs. 4-6 p.m.	Pay as you wish

If you have a whining child on your hands and you're down on the Lower West Side of Manhattan, make a stop at the Children's Museum of the Arts. A combination of museum and workshop, this place is designed to make any child happy—and as a result, adults, too.

While were there, the exhibition featured was that of Herb Williams, an artist who works with thousands of crayons that he turns into sculptural forms that are both beautiful and meaningful. Called *Beneath the Surface*, it consisted of colorful fish forms that have adapted to man-made ecological disasters. A blackfin tuna, meant to call urban sprawl to mind, was made with blue, tan, and black crayons that looked like a city. Another fish, a king salmon with an orange top and black bottom represented an oil slick, and a pike portrayed the colors of wildfire: yellow, orange, and red with small blue areas. The lesson was what an artist can do with a bunch of Crayola crayons.

A studio was furnished with low, round tables offering buttons, straws, paint, crayons, and more to energize the imagination of the young. Young adults oversaw the creative play of the children. We passed a table outfitted with green, sticky stuff, and one youngster was having a great time spreading it around. The sign above this art station said "Flubber—have fun, please share, but beware, Flubber will stick to your clothes and hair." The space was decorated by large framed self-portraits made by the children. The bathrooms sported colorful images by Jamie Kelty based upon those by Keith Haring. Downstairs is a playroom. A young boy was having great fun bouncing and falling on large balls.

Also downstairs is the media lab, directed by film maker Joe Veno, where kids learn about animation and film-making. A large room is also available for birthday parties and other special events.

China Institute Gallery

Location and Transit
125 East 65th Street
(212) 744-8181
chinainstitute.org
Subway: 4, 5, 6, F, N, R
Bus: M66, M101, M102, M103

Hours and Admission

Mon., Wed., Fri.-Sun.	10 a.m.-5 p.m.	
Tues., Thurs.	10 a.m.-8 p.m.	
Adults		$7
Seniors and students with ID		$4
Members and children under 12		Free

For anyone interested in the history of Chinese-American relations, this small museum is a must. Behind gleaming red doors guarded by stone figures, the institute has an exhibit space on its main floor that presents Chinese art, architecture, sculpture, photography, and folk arts from the Neolithic period to the present century. The institute has been fostering cross-cultural understanding since 1926.

The museum features two major exhibitions per year, including traveling exhibitions. We saw a fascinating exhibit called *Humanism in China: A Contemporary Record of Photography*, which offered one hundred photographs from an estimated one hundred thousand documentary photos taken by one thousand photographers from all over China. The photos, taken between 1951 and 2003, offered an amazing glimpse into the ordinary lives of the Chinese people, inviting the gallery visitor to contemplate the extraordinary changes in Chinese society during the last half of the twentieth century.

The exhibition included a photo of a man on crutches wearing a sack inscribed "Vagrants Complaint" that proclaims his suffering as he goes begging, as well as a 1999 picture of a lucky man at the lottery, smiling widely, his arms loaded with bills. Particularly emotional was a photo of a man in Beijing holding a photo of his dead wife, fulfilling their dream of visiting Beijing together. We also saw photos of people in the traditional Mao outfits as well as later ones of young men and women in tight jeans and tighter blouses.

Past exhibitions touched on various topics, including *Confucius: His Life and Legacy in Art*, which offered related lectures on the life of Confucius and the three religions of China: Confucianism, Daoism, and Buddhism.

The China Institute has been chartered by the Board of Regents of the University of the State of New York as a school of continuing education and offers Chinese language courses for adults and children, a special Teach China program for educators, and a gallery tour program for organized groups called Discover China through Art. It also provides classes in Chinese painting and calligraphy, cooking, crafts, exercise, and a film series.

Cooper-Hewitt, National Design Museum

Location and Transit

2 East 91st Street
(212) 849-8400
cooperhewitt.org
Subway: 4, 5, 6
Bus: M1, M2, M3, M4

Hours and Admission

Mon.-Fri.	**10 a.m.-5 p.m.**
Sat.	**10 a.m.-6 p.m.**
Sun.	**12-6 p.m.**
Adults	**$15**
Seniors and students	**$10**
Children under 12	**Free**

The Cooper-Hewitt, National Design Museum of the Smithsonian Institution is housed in an impressive Fifth Avenue mansion that was built and owned by the late Andrew Carnegie. It is a special place because of the subtle tension created by the impressive modern objects it shows set within an old, elegant, and imposing edifice. When he commissioned the house in the late 1890s, Carnegie wanted a large, light-filled, but simple home for his retirement. However, today's visitor, given the opportunity to see part of the sixty-four-room home in which Carnegie lived, might question its simplicity.

The ornate bronze front doors introduce the visitor to a foyer that leads up steps to the imposing great hall. The great hall is elaborately paneled in oak that is topped by a silver metallic-painted burlap frieze. The ceiling is also of carved oak. The first floor originally contained the entertaining rooms and Carnegie's private suite. Now, these rooms are devoted to the design holdings of the Smithsonian.

The first room we entered had been Carnegie's all-golden music room, which held the Design USA exhibition commemorating the tenth anniversary of the National Design Awards. The exhibit featured the accomplishments of the seventy-five winners honored during the first ten years of the awards. This room held the first laptop computer, designed by Bill Moggridge; Milton Glaser's iconic Bob Dylan poster; and Lella and Massimo Vignelli's famous New York City subway map. It also honored Eva Zeisel, who, at the age of 102, was still designing. The exhibit continued through additional ornate rooms and featured such award winners as diverse as the Aveda Corporation for use of renewable resources, Nike for its Zoom Victory Spike, Yves Béhar for Birkis clogs, Target for "great design, everyday, for everyone," Tupperware, Robert Greenberg for interactive design through Ticketmaster, and Ralph Appelbaum Associates for the United States Holocaust Museum. It was an exciting exhibit full of the familiar and strange, all set against the paneled and gold-painted mansion walls.

The second floor, which contained the family bedrooms, is accessed by a grand wooden staircase from the great hall or an elevator. It now holds the museum's temporary exhibitions.

There is a small cafeteria and a lovely atrium eating area.

The Czech Center New York

Location and Transit
321 East 73rd Street
(646) 422-3399
new-york.czechcentres.cz
Subway: 6
Bus: M15

Hours and Admission
Sun.-Sat.   10 a.m.-6 p.m.
Free

Hidden away on the far east side of New York City—on East 73rd Street, to be exact—the Czech Center New York occupies a light stone building fronted by large pillars called the Bohemian National Hall. However, the Grecian style of the outside belies the care and artistry of its very modern interior.

The center is the home of the Czech Consulate General in New York, the Bohemian Community Center, the Bohemian Benevolent and Literary Association (a library largely in English), a beautiful ballroom, and a weekly summer rooftop cinema, as well as many programs for those interested in Czech culture, life, business, and tourism. Its aim is to provide increased understanding between the Czech Republic and the United States.

It also provides space for a large, one-room gallery, which features changing exhibits. We saw an exhibit called *Prague through the Lens of the Secret Police*. This show presented large photographs from the book of the same title published by the Institute for the Study of Totalitarian Regimes, located in Prague. These photographs were taken with hidden cameras during the hard-line socialist regime that followed the Soviet occupation of Czechoslovakia in 1968. These chilling photos, one taken from a baby carriage, were designed to provide incriminating evidence about Czech citizens who were opposed to the regime as well as their friends, families, and other acquaintances.

The Drawing Center

Location and Transit

35 Wooster Street
(212) 219-2166
drawingcenter.org
Subway: 1, 6, A, C, E, J, N, R, Q, Z
Bus: M5, M21

Hours and Admission

Wed., Fri.-Sun.	12-6 p.m.
Thurs.	12-8 p.m.
Mon.-Tues.	Closed
Adults	$5
Students and seniors	$3
Members and children under 12	Free
Thurs. 6-8 p.m.	Free

From the outside, the Drawing Center looks just about like any other art gallery in Soho. However, up a few decorative iron steps typical of the neighborhood and through a heavy door, a visitor meets a large exhibit space, unique in that this space is devoted only to the art of drawing, past and present. The center has a smaller annex across Wooster Street. The center also boasts a book shop, which purveys volumes about the exhibited artists and general books about drawing.

The day we were there, the main gallery was painted a beautiful, deep terra-cotta color, the better to display the drawings of Leon Golub mounted in white frames, each measuring 9" x 12". The exhibit, *Leon Golub: Live*

& Die like a Lion?, featured approximately fifty oil stick or acrylic and ink drawings on Bristol board and vellum that the artist created between 1999 and 2004. Known primarily as a painter preoccupied with the atrocities of the external world, these drawings are largely of a personal nature. However, many of the drawings bore texts, some of them humorous and others serious. For example, one drawing, titled the *American Girl*, was of a nude woman with red, white, and blue stars on her torso. Another abstract drawing bore a scrawled "I Do Not Bend Beneath the Yoke" under a shadowy figure. The exhibit also included an unfinished painting on a very large canvas, featuring a sketch of two lions.

Across the street, we encountered a different aesthetic. The exhibit *Dorothea Tanning: Early Designs for the Stage* contained costume sketches for George Balanchine ballets, including *The Night Shadow, Bayou, and Will-o'-the-Wisp*. These drawings were airy, light, impersonal, and often phantasmagoric. Enriching the exhibit were photographs of the actual costumes of performers which one could compare to the sketches Tanning made for them.

Whatever the exhibit, the Drawing Center is likely to intrigue and surprise.

n Iannis Xenakis: Composer, Architect, onary. *Photograph by Cathy Carver.* (Courtesy es Galleries)

From Iannis Xenakis: Composer, Architect, Visionary. *Photograph by Cathy Carver.* (Courtesy Forbes Galleries)

Dyckman Farmhouse Museum

Location and Transit

4881 Broadway
(212) 304-9422
dyckmanfarmhouse.org
Subway: 1, A
Bus: M100, BX7

Hours and Admission

Fri.-Sun.	11 a.m.-5 p.m.
Mon.-Thurs.	Closed
Adults	$1
Children under 10	Free

Surrounded by well-tended and lovely gardens, the white wooden building that is the Dyckman Farmhouse peeks out above a rise on busy northern Broadway. Built in approximately 1784, this Dutch Colonial-style home stood on what was then Kingsbridge Road and commanded a farm of 250 acres, the largest in Manhattan. In those early days, one could see from the East River to the Hudson from the windows inside this modest house. The farmhouse opened as a museum in 1916 and is now managed by the New York City Parks Department. The docents there are engaging and knowledgeable.

Tended in the 1790s by Jacobus, the great-grandson of the Dutch settler of the original land, Jan Dyckman, the farm flourished. It is believed that during this time, ten people lived in the house. They included Jacobus, three of his sons, his young grandson, his niece, one unidentified white woman, a free black woman, a free black boy, and one male slave. Thirty other people, including laborers and other Dyckman family members, lived in three other houses scattered around the farm.

During this time, there would have been a parlor and two bedrooms on the first floor. It is thought that Jacobus, who was in his seventies, occupied one bedroom, and his niece, Maria, the other small private room. One large space on the second floor offered sleeping accommodations for the other residents. Of the original farmhouse, only a few original artifacts remain, but the museum has a trove of treasures from archeological digs in the surrounding area of upper Manhattan. The museum keeps these interesting objects in the Relic Room on the first floor. There was both a summer and a winter kitchen. The winter kitchen would have kept the house warm during the cold weather and the summer kitchen was outside the main house so that it did not add to the heat in the rooms during the un-air-conditioned summer temperatures.

When the property was renovated by Dyckman descendents in 1915 and 1916, a reproduction of a stone smokehouse was built on the half-acre remaining to the house. The renovators also planted extensive gardens that today offer visitors color and scent during the growing season and an imaginative glimpse of what the farm might have looked like during its heyday. Residents of modern-day apartment houses on two sides of the rear garden can enjoy the plantings all year long.

It is a long trip to the very northern environs of Manhattan, so if you go it might be wise to combine a trip to the farmhouse with one to the Hamilton Grange National Memorial, which is a short bus ride south.

El Museo del Barrio New York

Location and Transit

1230 5th Avenue
(212) 831-7272
elmuseo.org
Subway: 2, 3, 6
Bus: M1, M2, M3, M4

Hours and Admission

Tues.-Sat.	11 a.m.-6 p.m.
Sun.	Closed
Adults	$9
Seniors and students	$5
Members and children under 12	Free
Wed.	Free for seniors

Everyone knows that New York City was and continues to be a melting pot. Waves upon waves of immigrants from all over the world have come to New York City to create a better life for themselves and their children. Many of these new Americans have created museums that celebrate their culture and history. El Museo del Barrio (literally, the Museum of the Neighborhood) is one of the best of these institutions. It honors the thriving and diverse Latino community in the city.

Recently renovated, with a stunning exterior facade and an exciting orange neon-lit lobby, the museum is located on upper 5th Avenue at 104th Street, the end of Museum Mile and the beginning of the Barrio, the Latino neighborhood in Spanish Harlem. It reopened in October 2009, its new space enlarged to display some of the sixty-five hundred objects collected since its inception in 1969 as well as fascinating special exhibitions.

We saw part of *Voces y Visiones: Four Decades through El Museo del Barrio's Permanent Collection.* It was a wonderful exploration of Latino art in the Americas, from the pre-Columbian Taíno culture, which flourished in Puerto Rico, the Dominican Republic, Haiti, Cuba, Jamaica, and the Bahamas between AD 1200 and 1500, to creative representations of modern Latino spiritual and cultural interpretation. We saw photos of migrant farm workers as well as devotional objects such as a primitive three kings sculpted out of wood by an unknown craftsman and *Vodun Banner depicting Saint James,* made from beads and sequins by Antoine Oleyant.

One of the most delightful exhibits was a wooden bed standing in the middle of the gallery. It was completely encrusted with all kinds of objects: ornaments of plastic and tinsel, small plastic baby dolls, toys, cars, a plastic snake coiled around the foot board, wedding cake toppers on the high posts. It sported a white satin bedspread covered entirely with tiny bows and objects commemorating various birthdays, christenings, marriages and other events. Called *La cama* (the Bed), it was created in 1987 by Pepón Osorio.

El Museo del Barrio has a wonderful, eclectic store that purveys objects, books, and jewelry from various Latino cultures as well as a light-filled cafeteria, where a visitor can lunch on tacos, chimichangas and other delicacies.

The Forbes Galleries

Location and Transit
62 5th Avenue
(212) 206-5548
forbesgalleries.com
Subway: 1, 4, 5, 6, 9, A, B, C, D, E,
   N, R
Bus: M1, M2, M3, M6

Hours and Admission
Tues.-Wed., Fri.-Sat.	**10 a.m.-4 p.m.**
Thurs.	**Group tours only**
Sun.-Mon.	**Closed**
Free	

The Forbes Galleries are a treat both for adults and children. Malcolm Forbes was a passionate collector in a variety of fields, and the evidence of his passion is on display on the ground floor of the impressive building named for the publication.

When we visited the museum, we saw the exhibit called *One Hundred Years of Toy Boats*. At its entry were the following words by Malcolm Forbes: "Toy boats were greatly prized by the children in the Forbes family. We were forever sailing them in nearby brooks and streams and in summers on lakes or oceans. Not a one survived to be part of this collection. But the memory of them and the joy of them accounts for its formation." And what a collection it was! Scores of warships sail on to imaginary encounters and we counted more than ninety ocean liners, big and little, plying a placid sea. The boats are of all sizes and of all types, including hand-painted specimens guaranteed to charm the onlooker of any age. In its own case was the wonderful *André*, the largest boat in the collection, driven by a powerful gas engine. On the walls were paintings of sea and sea-going vessels as well as a crayon drawing of a boat by Malcolm Forbes at age eight.

The exhibit *On Parade* offered hundreds of tin soldiers, cowboys, Indians, and other miniature tin figures meant to delight youngsters. This exhibit explained the beginnings of the little tin soldier in the region around Nuremberg, Germany, made by kitchenware and other tin workers, who used excess metal to form the small figures. The *Land of Counterpane* gave life to the famous Robert Louis Stevenson poem by recreating a children's sick room and the tin soldiers placed all up and down the ridges of the bed cover. Almost all the cases in this exhibit provided a step stool so that children could see as well as the adults.

There was plenty for adults to enjoy, including photographs from the Forbes Collection by photographers such as Harry Callahan, Lewis Hine, Robert Doisneau, Irving Penn, Alfred Stieglitz and Henri Cartier-Bresson. Another room featured a century's worth of costume jewelry, featuring sparkling samples of the work of Miriam Haskell and Hattie Carnegie, among others. Still another gallery exhibited artwork on women reading in a contemporary perspective.

The exhibits change frequently, but all are sure to delight both children and adults.

Courtesy Forbes Galleries

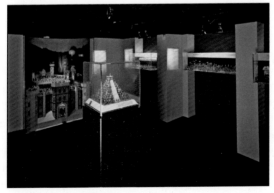

Courtesy Forbes Galleries

Fraunces Tavern Museum

Location and Transit

54 Pearl Street
(212) 425-1778
frauncestavernmuseum.org
Subway: 1, 4, 5, J, M, R, W, Z
Bus: M1, M6, M15

Hours and Admission

Sun.-Sat.	12-5 p.m.
Adults	$7
Seniors and children between 6 and 18	$4
Members and children 5 and under	Free

The red-brick building at 54 Pearl Street, the oldest public building in New York City, offers a front door entrance into Fraunces Tavern Museum. The charming structure was the original Fraunces Tavern, but the museum now consists of four colonial buildings creatively attached to the original, which together hold an impressive collection of American history. The five buildings are owned by the Sons of the Revolution in the State of New York, which saved the old Fraunces Tavern from destruction in 1904.

The original building dates back to 1719. It was built on land purchased by Stephen Delancey, who, according to records, planned to construct a large brick house—and evidently did just that. The building had several renters and owners during its earliest history but was ultimately sold to Samuel Fraunces, a tavern owner, in 1762. Fraunces called his business the Queen's Head Tavern, in honor of England's Queen Charlotte.

It was a smart buy for Fraunces, as it sat in the midst of the economic and political center of old New York, and it became one of the most popular taverns of its day. Although meetings were held at City Hall a few blocks away, many delegates ate well at the tavern after adjourning. John Adams wrote, after a banquet held there for the Massachusetts delegation to the First Continental Congress, "The most splendid dinner I ever saw, a profusion of rich dishes, etc." Fraunces Tavern still provides early American fare in the tavern that it leases to and is managed by professional restaurateurs. After the Revolutionary War, George Washington bid goodbye to his officers at Fraunces Tavern in the Long Room, the original tavern, which is still fitted as a Colonial restaurant. Col. Benjamin Tallmadge recorded the dramatic event: "Such a scene of sorrow and weeping I had never before witnessed."

In another gallery, one can see a brown lock of Washington's real hair as well as a piece from one of his teeth (which were not made of wood).

The museum offers an incredible heritage to visitors not only in its very bricks but also in its holdings. In the Gallery of Heroes, a visitor can see the famous painting by Dennis Malone Carter, *Molly Pitcher at the Battle of Monmouth*, as well as portraits of other famous Revolutionary War figures. The Flag Gallery holds the colorful flags of the various Revolutionary War regiments. We also saw a replica of the Magna Carta in that room. One can also see the Revolutionary War paintings of John Ward Dunsmore, who was a member of the Sons of the Revolution, as well as scores of documents related to the turmoil in the America of the day. In addition, the museum offers evening lectures about various themes and topics related to the American Revolution. A visit to Fraunces Tavern is a real trip back in time.

Courtesy Fraunces Tavern Museum

French Institute/Alliance Française

Location and Transit
22 East 60th Street
(212) 355-6100
fiaf.org
Subway: 4, 5, 6, E, N, R
Bus: M1, M2, M3, M4, M5, Q31

Hours and Admission

Tues.-Fri.	**11 a.m.-6 p.m.**
Sat.	**11 a.m.-5 p.m.**
Sun.-Mon.	**Closed**
Free	

If you find yourself shopping on the mid-Upper East Side among the luxury emporia, you might enjoy a peaceful and enlightening hour at the the French Institute/Alliance Française. Known for all levels of French instruction as well as French cultural activities, the institute also offers a small but refreshing gallery.

We saw the show *Paris/New York: Crisscross Views*, which featured different artistic perspectives of the two cities: Paris as it was photographed by American photographers and images of New York City by French photographers. Since the 1980s, the city of Paris has commissioned three prominent American photographers, Duane Michals, Bruce Davidson, and Ralph Gibson, to document the City of Lights. The French photographers, Raymond Depardon, Jeanloup Sieff, and Bernard Pierre Wolff, focused not so much on the sights and monuments of New York but more on the daily life of the people who live there.

On the Staten Island Ferry was a moving photograph in black and white by Raymond Depardon. It featured the ferry in the rain, commuters' umbrellas unfurled, and a hazy image of Manhattan in the fog. Jeanloup Sieff caught a reflection of a taxi in a side view mirror. Superimposed on this image were the wings of a Cadillac. Bruce Davidson provided an image of the iconic Eiffel Tower as it was seen through the branches of a tree. He also presented an allée (walkway) in a Parisian park with marvelous light peeking through the leaves and branches of the trees.

The gallery features changing exhibitions that detail all aspects of French and Francophone communities. The institute has a small shop but no eating area. However, there are many restaurants at all prices in this area of Manhattan and plenty of shopping opportunities.

The Frick Collection

Location and Transit

1 East 70th Street
(212) 288-0700
frick.org
Subway: 6
Bus: M1, M4

Hours and Admission

Tues.-Sat.	**10 a.m.-6 p.m.**
Sun.	**11 a.m.-5 p.m.**
Mon.	**Closed**
Adults	**$18**
Seniors	**$15**
Students with ID	**$10**
Sun. 11 a.m.-1 p.m.	**Pay what you wish**
Children 10 and under	**Not admitted**

The Frick Collection is housed in another of the magnificent former residences that are found along the length of Fifth Avenue. This impressive building, finished in 1914, belonged to Henry Clay Frick, who made his fortune in fuel and steel and used his wealth to acquire an extensive collection of art. After the death of Mrs. Frick in 1931, the architect John Russell Pope made changes and additions to the building, and in 1935, the collection was opened to the public.

The elegant structure and the art complement one another, since the collection contains magnificent paintings by the likes of Velázquez, Vermeer, Constable, Turner, de la Tour, van Dyck, El Greco, and Titian, with a small number of pre-Impressionist and Impressionist works by artists such as Corot, Degas, Monet, and Renoir. These paintings hang in the elegant downstairs rooms of the redesigned mansion. The library, filled with first printings of books on art, is dominated by a portrait of Henry Clay Frick that hangs above the fireplace. A portrait of lovely Mrs. Frick stands on a beautiful, wooden French desk. The room is graced by tall Chinese ceramic vases. Underfoot are priceless Oriental rugs.

The former dining room is graced by full-length portraits of women by Gainsborough, a reflection of the Gilded Age taste of Henry Clay Frick. The room, decorated in the English style, as it was in Frick's day, also holds a large painting of the Mall in St. James Park, also by Gainsborough in.

The east corridor holds mid-sized portraits, landscapes, and genre paintings from the eighteenth and nineteenth century, while one room exhibits a series of large wall panels painted by Fragonard of children engaged in adult work. It is called the Children's Room.

For a short rest, a visitor can sit on a marble bench in the Garden Court, surrounded by a garden of white foliage and flowers and soothed by the sound of a fountain.

When we were there, we saw a special exhibit called *Masterpieces of European Painting from Dulwich Picture Gallery*. The Dulwich Picture Gallery is the oldest public art gallery in England, founded by bequest to the boys' school Dulwich College by the art dealer and painter Sir Peter François Bourgeois. This exciting exhibit was graced by a marvelous painting, *A Girl at a Window*, by none other than Rembrandt.

Self-Portrait, c. 1658. Oil on canvas. By Rembrandt Harmensz van Rijn. Photograph by Michael Bodycomb. (Courtesy the Frick Collection)

Mistress and Maid, c. 1666-67. Oil on canvas. By Johannes Vermeer. Photograph by Michael Bodycomb. (Courtesy the Frick Collection)

The West Gallery. Photograph by Michael Bodycomb. (Courtesy the Frick Collection)

The Gabarron Foundation: Carriage House Center for the Arts

Location and Transit
149 East 38th Street
(212) 573-6968
gabarronfoundation.org
carriagehousecenter.org
Subway: 4, 5, 6, 7, S
Bus: M101, M102, M103

Hours and Admission

Mon.-Fri.	9 a.m.-5 p.m. by appointment
Sat.-Sun.	Closed
Free	

The Gabarron Foundation is both an easy miss and a complete surprise. If you walk along East Thirty-Eighth Street between Lexington and Park Avenues, you might stop to admire an impressive, old, three-story brick carriage house with large, forbidding wooden doors and a small bronze wall plaque designating it a heritage site. There is nothing to hint at the wonders inside.

This former carriage house and horse stable was built in 1902 by architect Ralph S. Townsend for his client William R. H. Martin. During its more recent history, it had been fully refurbished as a modern home, and then, under the aegis of the New York Heritage Preservation Commission, twenty-six hundred square feet became an exhibition and cultural space. In the entryway remain the original wooden doors that led to the horse stalls, and at the end of the first floor room is a small indoor garden space.

Spanish artist Cristobal Gabarron opened it as the American outpost for his Gabarron Foundation in order to foster the understanding of Spanish culture in the United States. It is an exciting space for Spanish and Latin American art.

The first floor is dominated by a cantilevered spiral staircase that reaches up all the way to the third floor. In addition, the first floor hosts the current exhibition, which changes every two months. When we were there, we saw the large sepia architectural canvasses of Javier Riaño, which communicated peace, solitude, and, often, loneliness. These paintings were hung dramatically on the stark white walls. The second floor is even more eye popping. Its large floor is covered with white tiles, and it flaunts a grand fireplace surrounded by copper. The entire ceiling of this floor is glass, and so the area is washed with incredible light. On the walls were the exciting canvasses of the permanent collection painted by Gabarron himself. The third floor, also approached from the spiral stair, constituted a balcony surrounding the light-filled floor below. It contained exhibit space and offices as well as a charming outdoor balcony. Our guide also showed us the shining stainless steel restaurant kitchen and what had been the bedroom of the house, replete with an oversized walk-in closet, a large Jacuzzi, and a state of the art bathroom.

The foundation changes its exhibits every two months. The extraordinary space also serves as an event venue.

German Consulate New York

Location and Transit
871 United Nations Plaza
(212) 610-9700
germany.info
Subway: 4, 5, 6, 7, S
Bus: M15, M50

Hours and Admission

Mon.-Fri.	**9 a.m.-12 p.m.**
Sat.-Sun.	**Closed**
Free	

If you are in the area of the United Nations—and most visitors to New York go to these notable buildings on the far east side of Midtown—it might be enjoyable to include a visit to the Consulate General of Germany a few blocks away. The only thing needed for entry is an entrance scan of yourself and your belongings.

When we were there, we saw a number of astonishing works of art. The centerpiece was a very large triptych by Simon Dinnerstein, measuring fourteen feet in width and seven feet in height. Begun in 1971, when the artist participated in a Fulbright Grant in Germany, he finished the masterpiece in 1974 in his Brooklyn studio. Dinnerstein has described *The Fulbright Triptych* as "the best possible of me times a hundred." Roberta Smith, writing in the *New York Times,* noted, "The work has the majestic symmetry and stillness of a religious altarpiece, and the intimate allure of a well-kept artist's studio. The object of worship is primarily art: old and new, high and low, in various mediums and styles." The triptych consists of two portraits on each end, one of the artist and the other of his wife. On the wife's lap is a baby, who did not exist when the painting was begun in Germany. A table in the center painting is laden with a variety of the artist's tools. On all of the plain pine walls are pinned postcards and cut-outs of the works of many different artists, and through two windows, one can see the small German village where the artist lived. Smith wrote that this was a painting that should not be missed.

Though *The Fulbright Triptych* was the most famous art work on hand, there were others that merited a visitor's interest. In the gallery upstairs, entered by a circular staircase or an elevator, was the exhibit *90 Days of Berlin* by Zigi Ben-Haim. Ben-Haim, an American Israeli artist, was invited to Berlin in 2004 as part of an Arts and Media program. It was his first trip to Berlin, and he painted a picture each day of his visit, forming a diary of his impressions of the city. In addition to the small "diary entries," there were two large oil paintings of Berlin as seen through the artist's eyes. In one, a blue animal kicked a soccer ball outside an important building out of which grew a very large rose. In the other, a small blue man rushed toward a very large banana, a common theme in his pieces.

Also on the first floor, we saw two very large, dark oil paintings and a series of three small, carved, wooden sculptures. Unfortunately, these works were accompanied by explanations in German that were not translated into English.

There is a small café, but it is unclear whether it is available to visitors.

Grey Art Gallery

Location and Transit

100 Washington Square East
(212) 998-6780
nyu.edu/greyart
Subway: 1, 6, A, B, C, D, E, F, M, N, R
Bus: M1, M2, M3, M5, M6

Hours and Admission

Tues., Thurs.-Fri.	**11 a.m.-6 p.m.**
Wed.	**11 a.m.-8 p.m.**
Sat.	**11 a.m.-5 p.m.**
Sun.-Mon.	**Closed**
Suggested admission	**$3**
NYU students, faculty, and staff	**Free**

The Grey Art Gallery is a small, provocative gallery located in Greenwich Village, in New York University's Silver Center. Just across the street from Washington Square Park, it is an open, well-lit space that shows the art to its best advantage. The gallery mounts its exhibits on two floors that are accessible to disabled visitors who request an elevator pass at the information desk. A pass is also required to approach and use the rest rooms on the second floor.

The day we visited, the Grey Art Gallery offered two intriguing exhibits. The first, on the street floor, was called *Concrete Improvisations: Collages and Sculpture by Esteban Vicente*. Vicente was an integral member of the New York School of painting, and, like his comrades, he explored color, form, and texture. Critics of his day called him a pioneer of action collage. Using torn paper, paint, and graphite, he created exquisite and interesting collages as well as vivid, colorful paintings. He was the only Spanish-born artist of the original Abstract Expressionists, having moved to the United States in 1936. Some of his earlier work consisted of black squiggles on white paper. When, in 1956, he began to incorporate all kinds of familiar food and machine labels into his work, the collages began to take on excitement and meaning. During his time as artist in residence at the Honolulu Academy of Arts, his collages and paintings were inspired by his surroundings, particularly the waters of the blue Pacific and the colorful vegetation that bordered it. These were quite beautiful. Also displayed were delightful small wooden sculptures which he had created from painted wood and cardboard scattered around his studio. They were fun to look at.

The second show in the basement gallery was called *Art • Memory • Place: Commemorating the Triangle Shirtwaist Factory Fire.* This exhibit was particularly meaningful, since one of New York University's buildings occupies the very site of the former Triangle Shirtwaist Factory, which burned on March 25, 1911, and killed 146 employees, mostly of whom were young women from Jewish and Italian immigrant families. *Art • Memory • Place* resulted from a collaboration between the Grey Art Gallery and graduate students in NYU's programs in museum studies and public history. The exhibit, which contained old photographs, including Lewis Hine's study of a child laborer; newspaper clippings; and other written materials, was an honorable memorial to those who died on that tragic day and a continuation of the request for the protection of worker's rights.

...rtesy James Prince

Courtesy James Prince

The Grolier Club

Location and Transit
47 East 60th Street
(212) 838-6690
grolierclub.org
Subway: 4, 5, 6, F, N, R, W
Bus: M1, M2, M3, M4, M57, Q32

Hours and Admission

Mon.-Fri.	**10 a.m.-5 p.m.**
Sat.-Sun.	**Closed**
August	**Closed**
Free	

Those who are interested in the art and history of the book as an object should certainly make a stop at the Grolier Club, which is easily accessible to those shopping or strolling on the Upper East Side. The club, in existence since 1884, has mounted more than eight hundred exhibitions on topics ranging from William Blake to Rudyard Kipling, from chess to murder mysteries, from Japanese prints to Art Nouveau posters. It was one of the first organizations in the United States to treat books and prints as objects worthy of display. The club mounts eight shows each year, four in the ground floor gallery and four in the second floor gallery.

Are you familiar with the 1941 movie *That Hamilton Woman,* starring Vivien Leigh and Laurence Olivier? It was based, somewhat loosely, on the life of Emma Hamilton, the subject of the Grolier Club's exhibit *The Enchantress: Emma, Lady Hamilton.* We were privileged to see it on our visit.

Lady Hamilton had an unusual life. Using her beauty and charisma, she rose from the lowly station of Amy Lyon, daughter of a country blacksmith, and reinvented herself as the glamorous Emma Hart while in her teens. The letters, papers, and photographs that document her extraordinary life were part of the Jean Kislak collection of manuscripts, books, and art related to Lady Hamilton and the era in which she lived. Emma Hart went to London, became a dresser at Covent Garden and parlayed her beauty to become an artist's model. She posed for Joshua Reynolds, Thomas Lawrence, John Hoppner, and Benjamin West. The more than sixty portraits painted by the obsessed George Romney made her famous and, indeed, immortalized her. Three of his paintings were in the exhibit, and her beauty and allure were unmistakable. By the time she was twenty-six, she had become the wife of Sir William Hamilton, the sixty-one-year-old British envoy to the court of Naples.

The second floor exhibit was fascinating also, but for completely different reasons. Called *Printing and the Brain of Man*, it featured old medical books from the collection of Eugene S. Flamm. It included the first illustrated textbook of anatomy published in England in 1545 and also featured a medical volume from Prussia dating from 1498, which included a woodcut of the brain by Albrecht Dürer.

The Hamilton Grange National Memorial

Location and Transit
414 West 141st Street
(646) 548-2310
nps.gov/hagr
Subway: 1, A, B, C, D
Bus: M3, M4, M5, M100, M101,
  BX19

Hours and Admission
Wed.-Sun.	**9 a.m.-5 p.m.**
Mon.-Tues.	**Closed**
Free	

The lovely and extensive house built by Alexander Hamilton is about two miles south of the Dyckman farmhouse. This grand structure, built on Hamilton's thirty-two-acre estate in upper Manhattan, is now located in St. Nicholas Park at 141st Street and Convent Avenue. The yellow, two-story house with white trimming, in the Federal style, was the only house Hamilton ever owned. It was designed as a country house for his family and was finished in 1802, only two years before Hamilton died as the result of a duel with Aaron Burr, his political rival. The house, called the Grange after Hamilton's grandfather's estate in Scotland, has been rehabilitated and is now managed by the National Park Service. It is as much a chronicle of his eventful life as it is a historical structure.

Born and orphaned on Nevis in the West Indies, Alexander Hamilton came to New York at age seventeen to study at King's College (now

Columbia University). During his short lifetime, he was a military officer, lawyer, and delegate to the United States Constitutional Convention. Most important, he became the first United States Secretary of the Treasury.

The ground floor of the house, which was originally the area for the kitchens and ironing rooms, now is the entry area and visitor's center. Here, a visitor can see documents and photographs pertinent to Hamilton's life along with the dramatic changes that Hamilton made to the new country's economy by establishing a central bank and initiating a common currency, the dollar. It was Hamilton's management that began to get the fledgling United States out of the horrific debt it had incurred by the Revolutionary War.

On the former first floor of the house are several of the recently refurbished rooms that were part of the living area during Hamilton's time. The light yellow walls and the floor-to-ceiling windows in the parlor make it sparkle with light. Five of the deep red parlor chairs are originals. The dining room holds an enormous table, set as if company were coming. The large silver epergne in the center of the table, which holds grapes and other fruit, was actually purchased by Hamilton for this home. The study, a smaller room painted a bright green, attested to the owner's status. Only the wealthy could afford paint in bright and bold hues at the time.

This historic house has bathroom facilities but no place for eating. However, there are many inexpensive restaurants on Broadway. There is a bookstore that also serves as a gift shop. It is a long trip to the very northern environs of Manhattan, so if you go you might think of combining a trip to the Grange with one to the Dyckman Farmhouse Museum, just about two miles north.

The Hebrew Union College-Jewish Institute of Religion Museum—New York

Location and Transit

1 West 4th Street
(212) 674-5300
huc.edu/museums/ny
Subway: 6, A, B, C, D, E, F, M, N, R, W
Bus: M5

Hours and Admission

Mon.-Thurs.	9 a.m.-5 p.m.
Fri.	9 a.m.-3 p.m.
Sun. (occasional)	10 a.m.-2 p.m.
Sat.	Closed

Free with government-issued photo ID

An afternoon in Greenwich Village eating, shopping, and people watching can be complemented by a visit to the Jewish Institute of Religion Museum at Hebrew Union College, which offers an airy, compact venue that presents art on themes that are both deeply Jewish and recognizably universal. It emphasizes the creativity of contemporary artists from North America and Israel who use their talents to explore Jewish values, identity, history, and spirituality.

The day we visited, we were able to see an exhibit that had not yet opened. Called *A Stitch in Jewish Time: Provocative Textiles*, the works we saw were humorous, sad, and thought provoking, and the large ground-floor space was overflowing with texture and color. All were either made of fabric or incorporated fiber as part of the presentation. We saw a many-hued tapestry called *The Creation* by Judy Chicago and Audrey Cowan.

Artist Laurie Wohl charmed us with *Peace Like a River* in shades of aqua, violet, and blue with stitched excerpts from Biblical texts, particularly Isaiah 66:72, "Behold I will extend peace to you like a river." We smiled at Greg Lauren's stitched paper statue *Bar Mitzvah Boy* and marveled at a wonderful Torah cover that employed gold thread embroidered on velvet. Estelle Kessler Yarinsky used lace appliqué, machine stitching, and hand stitching for a portrait of Gracia di Nasi, a sixteenth century Converso Jew. We were silenced by Carol Hamoy's *Ten Plagues*, ten tan vintage nurses' uniforms on a circular hanger that could be moved around. Each uniform was embroidered with a twenty-first century plague: infertility, bigotry, cancer, homelessness, heart disease, pollution, famine, war, AIDS, and drought. Yael Lurie and Jean-Pierre Larochette displayed a wonderful Torah reading table cover stitched in bright red and purple intertwined Stars of David. Andi Aronovitz showed a sad coat made of digital scans of antique ketubat (marriage contracts) sewn together. The piece, called *Coat of the Agunah* with its ketubat and hanging threads, referred to the many women locked in failed or abusive marriages whose husbands will not grant them a *get*, an Orthodox divorce decree.

The Hebrew Union College-Jewish Institute of Religion Museum mounts a significant exhibit twice a year. In the past, it has devoted its space to Judy Chicago, Isaac Bashevis Singer, and the artists who illustrated his books, prints by Paul Weissman, and spectacular maps created by many artists. It does not have a café or a shop, but beautiful objects are displayed throughout the lobby and these may be purchased.

Herbert and Eileen Bernard Museum of Judaica

Location and Transit

1 East 65th Street
(212) 744-1400, ext. 259
emanuelnyc.org/museum.php
Subway: 4, 5, 6, F, N, R, W
Bus: M1, M2, M3, M4, M18, M66, M72

Hours and Admission

Sun.-Thurs.   10 a.m.-4:30 p.m.
Fri.-Sat., Jewish holidays   Closed
Free

This museum is a part of Temple Emanu-El, one of the largest Reform Jewish congregations, as well as the third oldest in the United States. Founded in 1845, it is not surprising that over the course of its existence it has collected an astonishing array of Jewish ceremonial and commemorative objects that it lovingly houses. Supervised and catalogued by a professional museum director, the beautiful artistic holdings of the temple are categorized into objects used in the sacred service, commemoratives, and objects for the home.

Among the sacred objects were breathtakingly beautiful Torah ornaments, such as the Schiff set made of gilded silver, embossed and chased with castings, enameling, lapis, and semi-precious stones. It has a three-dimensional crown set with rubies, lapis beads, and sapphires. Other Torah ornaments bore gilded bells and exquisite molding, and silver gilt Torah shields contained relief molding and scrollwork. One, called a Paris-Style Torah Shield was made of heavy silver in a rectangular form and was embellished by lions holding the Tablets of the Law (the Ten Commandments). This section also included Torah pointers (*yadaim*—to help the reader, who cannot touch the Torah with bare hands, follow the text) formed into birds' beaks and a pointing finger. There were also beautifully embroidered Torah curtains, binders, and wonderfully made brass Hanukkah menorahs.

To honor people for their achievements and service to the synagogue, it is customary for congregations to give them special gifts. Often these gifts are returned to the synagogue as bequests, and Temple Emanu-El has many such objects. These include silver ceremonial wine goblets, embossed trays, intricately wrought vases of many sizes, bowls, ceremonial keys, cups, and medals.

Some of the more interesting objects in this museum of Judaica were objects made for home use and then donated to the temple. These included Bibles enclosed in delicate silver bindings with engravings of the Tablets, miniature Torah pointers, and a decorated Kiddush cup made of red glass. Hanging lamps of silver, gilt, and brass that once adorned a Jewish home joined other Sabbath lamps and delicate filigree spice towers. There were decorated charity boxes and beautiful mezuzah covers as well as clothing worn by Jews in Bokhara and Morocco. Also fascinating were old printed documents including deeds to pews and cemetery plots and a *mohel's* book of instructions for circumcision.

Anyone even slightly interested in Jewish history will be entranced by a visit to this museum—and, don't forget to pay a visit to the lovely synagogue while you're there.

The Hispanic Society of America

Location and Transit
613 West 155th Street
(212) 926-2234
hispanicsociety.org
Subway: 1, C
Bus: M4, M5

Hours and Admission

Tues.-Sat.	**10 a.m.-4:30 p.m.**
Sun.	**1-4 p.m.**
Mon.	**Closed**
Free	

Way uptown on Broadway and 155th Street, we found a jewel of a museum. The Hispanic Society of America is one of the institutions ringing the lovely Audubon Terrace. The society was established in 1904 by an American scholar and philanthropist, Archer Millington Huntington, who, from an early age, was fascinated with Spanish culture and language. At nineteen, he expressed a desire to found a Spanish Museum. Today, the museum possesses the largest collection of Spanish paintings, decorative arts, sculpture, prints, photographs, books, and manuscripts outside of Spain and Latin America.

After we shed our outer garments in the small coatroom, we entered the panelled atrium, where we were greeted by a stunning painting by Goya, *The Duchess of Alba*, the most famous of this museum's significant Goya paintings and sketches. Also in the atrium was an exquisite, heavily carved drop-front secretary desk inlaid with ivory from the last quarter of the sixteenth century. Cases held silver religious objects, which included chalices, incense holders, and candelabras. On a wall surrounding the atrium was a wonderful altarpiece from 1550.

Adjoining rooms held wonders as well. In a room with a skylighted ceiling and a floor of red tile was a fourteen-part mural covering the four walls called *Vision of Spain*, by the painter Joaquín Sorolla y Bastida. These paintings envisioned various cultures and areas of Spain, including the Bullfighters in Seville, the Castile Bread Festival, the Aragon jota, and the Seville Dance. The room, shimmering with the bright colors of the paints, was spectacular. Another room contained funerary art, including entire tombs. The tomb of the Bishop of Palencia from the early sixteenth century was particularly eye catching. The downstairs also held splendid examples of ceramics, including apothecary jars, plates, and spice boxes from Spain and Mexico. Also present were door knockers from the 1500s, which used bird and animal forms in wonderfully wrought and creative iron work.

The upper level, a balcony surrounding the atrium, held a short survey of Spanish paintings from the sixteenth through the twentieth centuries. This gallery held paintings by El Greco, Velázquez, and Goya, along with many others. This gallery also held a portrait of Louis Comfort Tiffany from 1911.

Unfortunately, the Hispanic Society of America has no dining area, no elevators, and is not accessible for disabled individuals.

The Institute for the Study of the Ancient World

Location and Transit

15 East 84th Street
(212) 992-7818
isaw.nyu.edu
Subway: 4, 5, 6
Bus: M1, M2, M3, M4, M86

Hours and Admission

Tues.-Thurs.,	
Sat.-Sun.	**11 a.m.-6 p.m.**
Fri.	**11 a.m.-8 p.m.**
Mon.	**Closed**
Free	

The Institute for the Study of the Ancient World is a rich storehouse of information for anyone interested in antiquity and former civilizations. Past exhibits include *Echoes of the Past: The Buddhist Cave Temples of Xiangtangshan, Nomads and Networks: The Ancient Art and Culture of Kazakhstan,* and *Before Pythagoras: The Culture of Old Babylonian Mathematics.*

The day we visited, the Institute was featuring *Nubia: Ancient Kingdoms of Africa.* Now, we had heard of the Nubians, who were mentioned in a variety of our readings as children and adults, but we never knew exactly who they were. Nor did we know about the rich cultural and economic life that these ancient people lived.

The exhibit detailed everything from the geographic area of Nubia, located in what is now northern Sudan and southern Egypt in the Nile

Valley, to its history and culture. The men of Nubia were known and feared for their skill in archery. Thus, the earliest Egyptian term for the area was "Ta Seti," or "land of the bow." Records reveal that Nubians had substantial interactions with Egyptians, including exchanges of culture and trade. As part of the display, we saw representative pieces of Nubian craft and artwork, including a pitcher in the form of a hippopotamus, dated between 1700 and 1500 BC, and a beautiful, incised, convex black bowl created sometime between 1900 and 1750 BC. There was Faience made of crushed quartz or sand and finished with a lovely blue-green glaze. Since Nubians were usually buried with their jewelry, most objects that were displayed had been recovered from funeral sites and temples. Included in the collection were bas reliefs and statues, depicting Nubians with tightly curled hair and diagonal scars on their cheeks. Today, the Nubian population is divided between Egypt and Sudan.

The museum features one subject at a time and provides a very comprehensive overview of the topic.

Instituto Cervantes

Location and Transit
211 East 49th Street
(212) 308-7720
nyork.cervantes.es
Subway: 6, E, M, V
Bus: M50

Hours and Admission

Mon.-Fri.	**9 a.m.-6:30 p.m.**
Sat.-Sun.	**Closed**
Free	

Down a tunnel-like entry on East 49th Street, a visitor will find two enjoyable experiences. First is Amster Yard, a greenery-filled courtyard with benches, offering guests—particularly in warmer weather—a peaceful respite from the surrounding and hectic city. Second is Instituto Cervantes (the Cervantes Institute), renowned for its excellent Spanish language courses and also offering lectures, performances, films, and a small gallery for the Spanish and Spain loving among us.

When we visited the gallery, it offered *Los Mundos de Gonzalo Torrente Ballester,* or the *Worlds of Gonzalo Torrente Ballester.* Ballester was a beloved Spanish novelist who also was a clever and funny journalist, screen writer, historian, scholar, teacher, Falangist, political Leftist, and sometime photographer. The exhibit explored six parts of the life and interests of GTB, as he was called in the explanatory material: photographer, author (and novelist), teacher, award-winner, and traveler. Although some of the explanatory signage was in Spanish, the non-Spanish speaker could determine the content of the items on display.

GTB Photographer featured his largely domestic photographs of people and structures around the town of Serantes, Ferrol, in Galicia, where he was born. The Fantastic Trilogy celebrated this much beloved work through quotations and a case full of various printings of these books. Unfortunately, the explanatory signage was in Spanish. However, from the quotes and the cover art one realized that the trilogy was a work of magic realism. GBT in Albany offered documents and photos recalling his time at the New York State University in Albany, where he taught from 1966 to 1973 as that institution's first distinguished professor. GBT Novelist gave an insight into the man through his quotations. GBT and Cervantes celebrated Ballester's love of the famous author and his receipt of the prestigious Cervantes Prize. The Places of Gonzalo Torrente Ballester showed photos of the important places in his life, from his birthplace to his favorite drinking establishment.

The exhibitions tend to focus on one Spanish artist and change multiple times per year. The Instituto Cervantes offers visitors an illuminating time-out from the busy city that surrounds it.

International Center of Photography

Location and Transit

1133 Avenue of the Americas
(212) 897-0000
icp.org
Subway: 1, 2, 3, 7, A, B, C, D, E,
  F, M
Bus: M5, M6, M7, M42, M104

Hours and Admission

Tues.-Thurs.,	
Sat.-Sun.	10 a.m.-6 p.m.
Fri.	10 a.m.-8 p.m.
Mon.	Closed
Adults	$14
Seniors and students with ID	$10
Members and children	
under 12	Free
Fri. 5 p.m.-8 p.m.	Pay what you can

Located in the heart of New York City near Times Square, the International Center of Photography was established to explore the heart of photography in its myriad forms. It was founded in 1974 by Cornell Capa as a living memorial to four photographers who lost their lives in the 1950s while on photojournalism assignments: Robert Capa, Cornell's brother; Werner Bischof; David Seymour; and Dan Weiner. Since its founding, ICP has also become a recorder of trends and experiments in photography. If an individual is curious about what is happening in the world of photography and video, a visit to ICP would be very worthwhile. ICP is also home to a vibrant school, offering more than five hundred courses for photo enthusiasts, both novice and master.

The show *Perspectives 2010* featured the works of present-day photographers Matthew Porter, Carol Bove, Ed Templeton, and Lena Herzog. Some of it was interesting and some parts of the show were baffling, including a work by Carol Bove that featured a desk with wooden shelves filled with books and personal belongings. Also strange and compelling was Lena Herzog's *Lost Souls,* photographs of objects in sixteenth century Wonder Cabinets. These rooms, a precursor to modern-day museums, featured medical anomalies and bizarre objects put on display for a thrill-hungry public.

Another macabre exhibit featured the 1860s work of a Dutch physician, who modeled fifty mouse skeletons into an orchestra and chorus and called his work *Rhapsody in Death.*

Most compelling, however, was a large exhibit in the downstairs gallery, *For All the World to See: Race Relations in America.* It described itself as "visual culture and the struggle for civil rights" and was a comprehensive overview of visual images from the days of slavery and Jim Crow through the election of a black president. It included iconic images of signs barring blacks from drinking fountains, busses, restaurants, and restrooms in addition to images of lynchings. Also displayed were photographs of Martin Luther King Jr., the Black Panthers, and a little, pig-tailed black girl accompanied by FBI agents to her first day in a former whites-only school. It featured newspaper photos chronicling freedom marches and some catching horrible moments of police violence. It was all there, giving truth to the old saw that a picture is worth a thousand words.

Courtesy International Center of Photography

Courtesy International Center of Photography

International Print Center New York

Location and Transit
508 West 26th Street, 5th Floor
(212) 989-5090
ipcny.org
Subway: 1, C, E, F, L, M
Bus: M23

Hours and Admission
Tues.-Sat.   **11 a.m.-6 p.m.**
Sun.-Mon.   **Closed**
Free

The International Print Center New York (IPCNY) has been adhering to its primary goal of encouraging appreciation of and education about prints as art since 2000. In a large, white space, which overlooks the new extension and staircase of the Highline Elevated Park at 26th Street, it mounts four juried shows of new prints each year. In addition, it offers two shows annually that focus on prints from a particular period, culture, or workshop. It also provides a traveling exhibition program that loans fine prints to regional museums such as the Pearlstein Gallery at Drexel University in Philadelphia, the Davis Museum at Wellesley College in Massachusetts, and Wave Hill in New York.

We were fortunate to visit while the center was showing its juried exhibition *New Prints 2010/Winter.* We saw wonderful contemporary prints using many different techniques. One of the most eye-catching pieces was an installation by Tai Hwa Goh of three-dimensional prints covering four walls. *LULL-1, LULL-4, LULL-5* attracted, both by its very size and its technique. Fantasy marine subjects in brilliant colors conveyed an airy and ethereal beauty. The piece was an intaglio on hand-waxed paper and collage that were mounted on wood board. Other printmakers experimenting and exhibiting were Nicholas Brown with *Underbrush 24*, a linoleum cut, and Greg Darker, whose untitled work was a laser engraving with relief ink and spray paint on masonite. Carla Aspenburg showed a transfer ink print made from a shattered glass plate, using the broken plate as her matrix. Rosaire Appel in *Say When* offered a digitally printed fold-out book, held in a glass case, and Grainne Dowling showed *Wintering with Snow*, an etching.

A printed list of the exhibitors is available with information for interested viewers who may wish to purchase a print. The Print Center does not sell any prints except those they own, which also may be seen and purchased online. Also available for visitors is a glossary of print-making techniques, which can aid the viewer to appreciate the work in the gallery, and a listing of print workshops and contract printers in the New York area.

Because of the development of the High Line, many new restaurants have opened in the surrounding area.

International Standards of Excellence (ISE) Cultural Foundation

Keiko Miyamori: Bird Cages and the Gilded Boat, an installation with soundscape by Steven Berkowitz. January 14 - February 26, 2011

Location and Transit

555 Broadway
(212) 925-1649
iseny.org
Subway: N, R
Bus: M5

Hours and Admission

Tues.-Sat.	11 a.m.-6 p.m.
Sun.-Mon.	Closed
Free	

Even on a busy lower-Broadway commercial street, it is possible to temper the hectic shopping experience with a little culture. The ISE Cultural Foundation was established in 1983 through endowments by three large ISE Group companies: ISE America, Seaboard Foods, and Seaboard Farms. This cultural foundation, chaired by Hikonobu Ise, is largely devoted to the visual arts but has a most unusual approach to the art it shows. Instead of choosing the art, the foundation relies upon curators to propose a show and present it if chosen.

Through its Program for Emerging Curators, the foundation encourages curators to present cutting-edge artists of contemporary art in its two-thousand-square-foot gallery space. Through a formal competition held twice each year, the foundation asks emerging curators throughout the world to apply for the opportunity with a detailed proposal.

We were charmed to see *Keiko Miyamori: Bird Cages and the Gilded Boat*, an installation with soundscape by Steven Berkowitz, which was curated by Sean Stoops. The downstairs gallery is a generously sized white room containing four large white pillars. It was the perfect setting for the white-painted and elegantly scrolled iron bird cages that hung from the ceiling. Each cage had an open top, implying the basic desire for escape from confinement. Hanging from the ceiling in the center of the room was a white canoe covered with washi paper with charcoal (traditional Japanese art materials) and a gilded inside with gold leaf. On the walls surrounding these sculptures were a series of circular frames containing large tree rubbings done in charcoal on white washi paper. These tree rubbings were made from the many trees on five continents visited by the artist. Beneath the rubbings were field recordings of lovely birdsong. For us, visiting this gallery in midwinter, it was a peaceful forecast of spring.

Upstairs, in the Front Space entry gallery leading from the street, were the brightly colored paintings of Hai-hsin Huang which had been curated by Fan-en Zoe Chiu. This exhibit was called *Comfortably Numb.* The artist critically highlighted that which was absurd in several institutions, including hospitals, schools, and prisons.

This small jewel has an elevator but no place for eating. However, there are many restaurants all around it.

Italian American Museum

Location and Transit

155 Mulberry Street
(212) 965-9000
italianamericanmuseum.org
Subway: F, N, R, V
Bus: M103

Hours and Admission

Sat.	**11 a.m.-6 p.m.**
Sun.	**12-6 p.m.**
Mon.-Fri.	**Closed**
Free	

The Italian American Museum is a tiny gem for native New Yorkers and tourists who treasure their cultural heritage. Located in the heart of Little Italy, the place of beginnings for many Americans of Italian descent, it is a very small museum made from a bank originally owned by an Italian family.

Banca Stabile was founded in 1885 by Francesco Rosario Stabile. During its most fruitful years, the bank offered newly arrived immigrants from Italy all kinds of services in addition to a full range of banking. It provided a link to their families back in Italy, telegraph and postal services, steamship tickets, a notary public, and import-export services. It acted as a kind of Italian community center. The museum maintains the original tellers' cages and its large, floor-to-ceiling vault.

Very young by New York City museum standards, the Italian American Museum was established in 2001 after the successful exhibition *The*

Italians of New York: Five Centuries of Struggle and Achievement was held at the New York Historical Society between October 1999 and February 2000. The museum continues to dedicate itself to documenting evidence of the struggles of Italian Americans and their achievements and contributions to American society. It is still collecting objects for display, which now include an old scissor and knife grinder's pushcart owned by Pietro Mariani and a home sewing machine. It also holds memorabilia of the original Italian community, including objects from the first Italian police officer to join the New York City Police Department as well as materials devoted to the well-known fighter for justice Frank Serpico.

The museum features exhibits on loan. On the day we visited, we saw *Unmasked: The Story of the Venetian Carnival,* lovely photos taken in Venice in 2008 by Anita Sanseverino.

Your visit to the Italian American Museum may not be a long one. It does not have a café or bathrooms. However, famous Italian pastry shop Ferrara and all the pasta one can eat is just steps away.

The Japan Society

Location and Transit

333 East 47th Street
(212) 832-1155
japansociety.org
Subway: 4, 5, 6, 7, E, M. S
Bus: M15, M42, M50, M101,
   M102

Hours and Admission

Tues.-Thurs.	11 a.m.-6 p.m.
Fri.	11 a.m.-9 p.m.
Sat.-Sun.	11 a.m.-5 p.m.
Mon.	Closed
Adults	$12
Seniors and students	$10
Members and children under 16	Free
Fri. 6 p.m.-9 p.m.	Free

The Japan Society offers a very different environment from the rest of the city. The large entrance lobby is a peaceful space with a modern Japanese sensibility. A Zen water garden planted with bamboo and other greens graces a corner near a staircase made of wood and Plexiglas. A beautiful, free-form wooden bench by the sculptor Nakashima offers seating and the opportunity to quietly meditate. Whispering feels more appropriate than talking loudly.

The Japan Society celebrated its centennial in 2007. Established to improve understanding between the United States and Japan, the organization was largely in decline during WWII. After the war, John D.

Rockefeller revived the society by donating land for the present house and recruiting many other prominent supporters. Today, the Japan Society has three thousand square feet of gallery space, a 260-seat auditorium, and a smaller room for classes and meetings.

The society does not have a permanent collection but schedules visiting exhibits semi-annually that are gleaned from private collections in the US and Japan. We saw *Serizawa: Master of Japanese Textile Design,* a mind-blowing exhibit of stencil-dyed cotton and hemp books, wall hangings, screens, kimonos, and obis done in dramatic colors with incredibly complex repeated designs. Among its past offerings, the society has shown medieval Zen portraits, masterpieces of lacquer, bamboo sculpture, and a plethora of other arts and crafts works.

A trip to the United Nations, only two blocks away, can include a visit to this wonderful, small museum. If you go on a Wednesday, you can also browse for your lunch or dinner at the outdoor farmer's market on Forty-Seventh Street, since the Japan Society does not have a restaurant or a store. However, it does offer surprising and unusual bathrooms. The society also holds classes about Japanese language and culture and presents live performance events, films, conferences, and symposia.

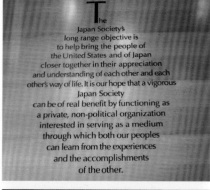

The Japan Society's long range objective is to help bring the people of the United States and of Japan closer together in their appreciation and understanding of each other and each other's way of life. It is our hope that a vigorous Japan Society can be of real benefit by functioning as a private, non-political organization interested in serving as a medium through which both our peoples can learn from the experiences and the accomplishments of the other.

The Jewish Museum

Location and Transit

1109 5th Avenue
(212) 423-3200
thejewishmuseum.org
Subway: 4, 5, 6
Bus: M1, M2, M3, M4, M86, M96

Hours and Admission

Sun.-Tues., Fri.-Sat.	11 a.m.-5:45 p.m.
Thurs.	11 a.m.-5:45 p.m.
Wed.	Closed
Adults	$12
Seniors with ID	$10
Students with ID	$7.50
Members and children 18 and under	Free
Sat.	Free

What a surprise this was! We had both visited the Jewish Museum many times in the past to explore various exhibits, however, neither of us had ever seen the permanent collection, an error we hope our readers will not make. The building, which had been a gift of his former home from banker Felix Warburg to the Jewish Theological Seminary, sits among the other mansions and great houses along Fifth Avenue. The banker's only stipulation in gifting the edifice was that the exterior or structure of the landmark building could not be changed in any way, and so it remains in its original facade.

We were led by a knowledgeable docent who took us to the fourth floor, which offered a stimulating exhibit called *Culture and Continuity: The Jewish Journey*. Here, we saw menorahs galore: some of them centuries old, others very modern, and even one created by Ludwig Wolpert in 1978. We visited a room filled with antiquities, including fertility idols. We traced the journey of the Jews from the Israelite Kingdom (1200-586 BCE) through the reigns of Saul, David, and Solomon. We saw artifacts from the Dura-Europos Synagogue, a frontier community in Syria. We were overwhelmed by a large selection of synagogue Hanukkah lamps and the descriptions of Hanukkah traditions among many nations. We saw a

Biedermeier wedding sofa and an Italian Torah ark in addition to displays pertaining to the various Jewish holidays and festivals. There was an entire room dedicated to Shabbat, with a table set for the Friday evening home service and meal, a cholent pot, and a variety of spice boxes.

The museum offered a twenty-eight-minute film about contemporary life in Israel, a section devoted to the Holocaust, and a gallery of contemporary Jewish artists, including Anselm Kiefer and George Segal. We saw a Robert Motherwell mural, Herbert Ferber sculptures, and a magnificent, colorful Torah curtain designed by Adolph Gottlieb. We were charmed by the exhibit of Curious George, the popular children's series created by Hamburg artists H. A. Rey and his wife, Margaret, who escaped the Holocaust through France, Spain, Portugal, and Brazil and landed in New York City in 1940. We were delighted that the museum had created a colorful space with many floor pillows on which children sat and lounged, reading about the wonderful monkey. It was a great visit.

There is a café featuring certified kosher fare and a wonderful shop selling Judaica, both serious and humorous.

ors to Culture and Continuity: The Jewish Journey. to right: The Holocaust *(1962), by George Segal;* Die Ɪmelspalaste *(2004), by Anselm Kiefer. Photograph*)*avid Gordon.* The Holocaust © *George and Helen* ꞮꞮ *Foundation/VAGA, New York.* (Courtesy The ꞮꞮ Museum)

Suite of sculpture and ceremonial objects, 1957: Creation *(wall sculpture/bimah screen) (1956-57), by Ibram Lassaw;* Torah Ark *(1956), by Philip Johnson and Ibram Lassaw;* Eternal Light *(1956-57), by Ibram Lassaw;* Bimah Chairs *(1956), by Philip Johnson. From Congregation Kneses Tifereth Israel, Port Chester, New York. Photograph by John Aquino.* (Courtesy The Jewish Museum)

Korean Cultural Service

Location and Transit

460 Park Avenue, 6th Floor
(212) 759-9550
koreanculture.org
Subway: 4, 5, 6, E, N, Q, R, V
Bus: M1, M2, M3, M4, M30, M31,
**   M57, M101, M102, Q32**

Hours and Admission

Mon.-Fri.   10 a.m.-5 p.m.
Sat.-Sun.   Closed
Free

Korean Cultural Service is not strictly a museum. It is a branch of the Ministry of Culture and Tourism of the Republic of Korea. Its mission is to promote cultural exchange and stimulate interest in Korean culture. The Korean Information Center contains more than sixteen thousand volumes on various aspects of Korean life and society. It also owns a broad collection of Korean films on DVD, hanbok (Korean traditional dress), and Korean musical instruments, all of which are available for borrowing.

The gallery at the Korean Cultural Service is a generous space that incorporates state-of-the-art lighting and environmental control. Gallery Korea is a site of cultural exchange between Korean and Western art lovers. Each year, it presents exhibitions devoted to contemporary art by Koreans living in Korea as well as those who live and work in other countries. It also mounts group shows featuring international artists.

We saw *Real in Transforum*, which featured the somewhat esoteric work of seven emerging architects. The exhibit was based on the idea that the world is perceived differently by each person, that the world is constantly changing because of changing technologies, and that architecture evolves by responding to the metamorphosis and is transformed by developments in other fields. The goal was for the architects to answer and demonstrate what the real is to them and their architecture. The exhibit displayed large video installations produced by the architects Jinpyo Eun, Jinwoo Heo, Ji Young Kim, Kyung Jae Kim, Sieun Lee, YeaHwa Kim, and Yong Ju Lee. The video installations were amazing examples of what advanced space and computer technology are capable. We saw swirling images of interlocking circles, buildings of steel designed from mapping the bark of trees, an open zoo, a wired community, and other complex images. Unfortunately, we felt that this presentation did not give us enough information to completely understand what the architects were conceptualizing.

The center also had a lovely decorated room that could have been dated anytime during the Chosŏn period, from 1392 to 1910. Called a sarangbang, this room is the equivalent of a living room crossed with a meditation space. It would be wonderful for any modern-day individual.

Kosciuszko Foundation

Location and Transit
15 East 65th Street
(212) 734-2130
thekf.org
Subway: 6
Bus: M1, M2, M3, M4

Hours and Admission

Mon.-Fri.	9 a.m.-5 p.m.
Sat.-Sun.	Closed
Free	

The Kosciuszko Foundation is headquartered in the lovely 1917 Van Alen mansion. It is dedicated to promoting understanding and friendship between Poland and the United States. The foundation is named in honor of Thaddeus Kosciuszko, a Polish general and patriot who, after unsuccessful battles in the uprising for Polish freedom, joined and the fight for American independence. The organization was founded in 1925, on the eve of the 150th anniversary of Kosciuszko's enlistment in the American liberation cause.

While the foundation is engaged in many activities supporting its mission, including scholarships, exchange programs, English instruction in Poland, and cultural programs across the nation, it also possesses an extensive collection of art by Polish painters and sculptors.

A beautiful, paneled second-floor room is used for lectures, films, and musical entertainment and displays many selections from its holdings. *Sculptures by Tracy H. Sugg* celebrated the features of major Polish figures, including Copernicus, Paderewski, Pulaski, and, of course, Kosciuszko. A very large painting above the fireplace dominates the room. *Kosciuszko at West Point* bears a small shield that contains words attributed to George Washington, "Kosciuszko is a man of science and merit." Other paintings by prominent Polish artists hang on the walls. *Poet's Sweetheart* by Leon Wyczółkowski and *Woman in Blue* by Olga De Boznanska were particularly appealing. In the paneled downstairs dining room is another Sugg sculpture of Marie Curie.

If you are interested in seeing current Polish art, the marble entry rotunda flanked by a sweeping staircase is the site for rotating art exhibits. We saw the paintings of Krystyna Brzechwa, a 1928-born artist who imparts a mystical, folk-like quality to her work. Her colorful, simple paintings depicted life in the Polish countryside as well as Polish folk tales and stories.

Merchant's House Museum

Location and Transit

29 East 4th Street
(212) 777-1089
merchantshouse.com
Subway: 6, B, F, N, R
Bus: M1, M5, M6, M103

Hours and Admission

Thurs.-Mon.	**12-5 p.m.**
Tues.-Wed.	**Closed**
Adults	**$10**
Seniors and students	**$5**
Members and children 12 and under	**Free**

If you are curious about what life was like for the upper middle class in New York City during the nineteenth century, then the Merchant's House Museum should be on your itinerary. It is the only house of its kind in New York that still has its original furnishings. Owned by Seabury Tredwell, who lived in it with his family, this house gives a visitor a glimpse into the kind of life they led.

We began our self-guided tour of the house on the lower floor in the kitchen, which would have been the workplace of the cook and the cook's helper. There, one can see the original cast-iron stove, the baking niche in a beehive oven, a pump for water, and a well-used wooden table. Outside the kitchen was the garden, which held the four-thousand-gallon cistern that fed water into the kitchen and provided water for washing upstairs as well. Many lovely shrubs and plants were recent plantings, although the bluestone path around the garden is original.

The first floor holds the parlor and the rear or dining parlor. The dining parlor contains a velvet settee, a mahogany dining table and sideboard, and twelve balloon-back chairs similar to the Duncan Phyfe style from around 1835. Because we were in the house in October, the main parlor was graced by an elaborately dressed coffin. Every fall, the museum reimagines the death and funeral of the patriarch, Seabury Tredwell. Funerals of the time were preceded by a short home ceremony attended by good friends and family. This room was lit by a bronze gas chandelier and a massive gilt mirror reflected its light. A Roman-design rug in colors of red, yellow, white, and blue covered the floor. Whale oil glass lamps shed meager light from on top of the coal fireplace's mantle.

Upstairs, we saw the bedroom occupied by the lady of the house, Elizabeth Tredwell. It was common for the men and women to have separate bedrooms at the time. In Elizabeth's room, there stood an additional small canopied bed to accommodate a sick child.

The master bedroom astounded us with the sound of dripping water coming from the vicinity of the large bed. We learned that this sound approximated the sound of melting ice, historically used to keep a corpse reasonably fresh (particularly during warmer weather). This demonstrates the level of detail and authenticity the museum employs to create a genuine experience for its guests.

We will never forget the dripping water that made our visit seem quite real.

The Morgan Library and Museum

Location and Transit

225 Madison Avenue
(212) 685-0008
themorgan.org
Subway: 4, 5, 6, 7, B, D, F, Q
Bus: M2, M3, M4, Q32

Hours and Admission

Tues.-Thurs.	10:30 a.m.-5 p.m.
Fri.	10:30 a.m.-9 p.m.
Sat.	10 a.m.-6 p.m.
Sun.	11 a.m.-6 p.m.
Mon.	Closed
Adults	$15
Seniors, students with ID, and children 12-16	$10
Children 12 and under	Free
Fri. 7 p.m.-9 p.m.	Free

When you visit the Morgan Library and Museum, be prepared for splendor as well as enlightenment. This museum has a split personality, one of the original library of the fabulously wealthy banker and collector J. Pierpont Morgan, the other of a modern glass structure displaying part of his vast collection.

The library wing consists of Italian Renaissance eye candy. Morgan's personal office, the librarian's office, and the library are filled with glowing brass, red silk damask, deep carpeting, a grand grey marble fireplace, Italian wooden objects, glass, and paintings by Renaissance masters, including Domenico Tintoretto and Hans Memling. The rotunda, to which the three rooms are attached, was the original entrance to the library and is constructed from white and beige marble and mosaic.

The library is amazing, filled with leather-bound books safely enclosed behind wire-fronted wooden cabinets and brass railings. And what books! The library owns three original Gutenberg Bibles, two printed on paper and one printed on vellum, one of which is displayed for the public.

Not to be missed is a twenty-minute film introduction to the man and his library, presented in the auditorium on the second floor. Morgan was an avid collector of drawings and prints, twenty-four thousand of them spanning the fourteenth through the twentieth centuries; printed books and bindings; medieval and Renaissance manuscripts, covering ten centuries of Western illuminated art; literary and historical manuscripts; ancient near-eastern seals and tablets; and music manuscripts, which include original handwritten works by Bach, Brahms, Mozart, Schubert, and Stravinsky, among others.

Courtesy Morgan Library and Museum

The museum also features changing exhibits. We saw *A Woman's Wit: Jane Austen's Life and Legacy.* We read some of her letters to her sister and others and learned that she self-published *Sense and Sensibility,* her first book. In addition to the exhibit, we also saw beautiful illuminations on some of the manuscripts from the Flanders area from the era of Catherine of Cleves. Included in this display were several very small books featuring breathtakingly tiny illustrations.

Courtesy Morgan Library and Museum

There are two dining places within the museum and a shop.

Courtesy Morgan Library and Museum

Morris-Jumel Mansion

Location and Transit

65 Jumel Terrace
(212) 923-8008
morrisjumel.org
Subway: C
Bus: M2, M3, M18, M101

Hours and Admission

Mon.-Tues.	By appointment only
Wed.-Sun.	10 a.m.-4 p.m.
Adults	$5
Seniors and students	$4
Members and children 12 and under	Free

In the upper reaches of the city is the oldest home in Manhattan, the Morris-Jumel Mansion, which was built in 1765 by British colonel Roger Morris as a summer home in the country. Originally surrounded by 130 acres of land, the open country acreage no longer exists, as every inch is prime in modern New York City.

The home itself has a history of interesting residents. Roger Morris married Mary Philipse, an American, and the two were among the wealthiest couples in New York at the time. They remained at the mansion for ten years, and the house was chosen as the headquarters for George Washington during the battle of Harlem Heights. Visitors can see Washington's bedchamber and marvel at the very short bed in which the big man slept. (At the time, it was thought that it was healthier to sleep in a sitting position, which explains the length of the bed.)

During the revolution, the mansion and land was seized and sold from the Morris family, who were loyal to Britain. It later served as an inn owned by a succession of inn keepers. However, in 1810, it was restored to its original purpose as a home by Stephen Jumel, a French immigrant, and his wife, Eliza. Stephen died in 1832, and Eliza, then one of the wealthiest women in New York, later married Aaron Burr, the former US vice president. The marriage took place in the parlor of the mansion, and after Burr's untimely death in a famous duel, Eliza retained ownership of the home.

We were fortunate to have been shown around the house by the mansion's director of education, who was charming and possessed a wealth of knowledge. She took us first to the original kitchen in the basement, where visitors can see the kinds of utensils used at the time. The kitchen also contains the original beehive oven, where all baking and cooking took place. On the first floor, we admired the Octagon Room formerly used for entertaining, with walls graced with beautiful blue reproduction wallpaper. It was one of the earliest octagon shaped rooms in the colonies, its unusual shape providing better cross-ventilation and airflow. We saw the formal dining

room in which George Washington, then president of the fledgling country, returned in 1790 to dine with members of his cabinet. Guests at the table included three future presidents of the United States: John Adams, Thomas Jefferson, and John Quincy Adams. Alexander Hamilton and Henry Knox were at the event as well.

On the second floor we saw Eliza Jumel's sumptuous bedroom, that of Mary Bowen, Eliza's adopted daughter, and that which belonged to Aaron Burr. We also admired paintings of many of the mansion's owners and guests.

A visit to the Morris-Jumel Mansion is a wonderful, vivid trip through the early history of our country.

Mount Vernon Hotel Museum and Garden

Location and Transit	Hours and Admission	
421 East 61st Street	**Tues.-Sun.**	**11 a.m.-4 p.m.**
(212) 838-7225	**Mon.**	**Closed**
mvhm.org	**Adults**	**$8**
Subway: 4, 5, 6, F, N, R	**Seniors and students**	**$7**
Bus: M15, M31, M57	**Members and children**	
	under 12	**Free**

A wonderful anachronism, the Mount Vernon Hotel Museum with its lovely gardens is a delightful and charming old house made of bedrock surrounded by the high rise buildings typical of New York City. It is tucked away on East Sixty-First Street, next door to the New York headquarters of the Colonial Dames of America, which protected the old hotel and now runs it.

The property was bought in 1795 by Abigail Adams Smith and her husband as a potential site for a vacation house. However, the Smiths lost the property to the bank, and William Robinson bought and improved the site. He built a large carriage house to accompany his mansion on present-day First Avenue. Visitors can still see the access road that was elevated up from the street to provide a home for the carriages and the horses that propelled them.

The carriage house began life as a day hotel in 1826. Far up into what was then the country from the crowded and hectic young New York City, which was located largely below Fourteenth Street, it provided a day's respite for its growing affluent population. Men and women who came to the hotel by stagecoach or ferry experienced a pleasant day in the country walking its extensive green grounds, splashing or boating in the nearby East River, and having a wonderful midday meal or tea at the hotel. There were a few rooms for those who preferred to stay overnight as well.

While little of the furniture in the building is original, it is all true to the period during which it functioned as a hotel. The dining room is set with plates and utensils used in the era, and a variety of cooked dishes on the bountiful board reflect the appetites and tastes of the time. Oysters were the hotdogs of the day, and the hotel was widely known for its turtle soup.

In each room, a visitor will find a book that explains all the furniture and fixtures within the room. These books will tell you about the French barrel organ in the parlor, the Japanning on the nineteenth-century floor clock, and the Staffordshire plates made in England for the American market that bear a transfer pattern of New York's City Hall. The garden at the back is a lovely retreat, even though the Fifty-Ninth Street Bridge looms overhead.

A visit to the Mount Vernon Hotel Museum is a refreshing step back into New York City history and can serve even present-day guests with a wonderful few hours of peace and tranquility.

Museum at Eldridge Street

Location and Transit
12 Eldridge Street
(212) 219-0302
eldridgestreet.org
Subway: 6, B, D, F, J, N, Q, R, Z
Bus: M15

Hours and Admission

Sun.-Thurs.	**10 a.m.-5 p.m.**
Fri.	**10 a.m.-3 p.m.**
Sat.	**Closed**
Adults	**$10**
Seniors and students	**$8**
Children aged 5-18	**$6**
Children under 5	**Free**

The Museum at Eldridge Street is based in the magnificently restored 1887 Eldridge Street Synagogue, a National Historic Landmark. Just blocks from the Lower East Side Tenement Museum, it urges us to understand a specific chapter in the living history of the United States—the enormous influx of millions of Eastern European Jews to the Lower East Side.

The Museum at Eldridge Street offers one-hour guided tours given by docents who really know their history. The tour begins with an overview of the development of the synagogue, which was opened in 1887 by a group of successful Orthodox Eastern European Jews. They wished to show the already ensconced German Jews that the Jews from Eastern Europe could create a building of stunning beauty through which their culture would flourish in America. And that is exactly what they did. The synagogue was designed by the Herter Brothers Architectural firm, even though they were not Jewish. (This may account for the trefoil design on the synagogue pews.)

For its first forty years, the synagogue was sustained by a vital Lower East Side community who gathered to celebrate holidays, mark life cycle events, hear gossip, and discuss community issues. However, by the 1920s, most of the original congregants had become economically mobile and had moved away from the Lower East Side, just as had the groups before them. During the 1950s, the remaining small group of congregants who worshipped in the street-level chapel could no longer afford repairs and heating, and the marvelous building fell into serious disrepair. The synagogue remained closed for twenty-six years.

Today, through the work of the Eldridge Street Project, an independent restoration not affiliated with any institution or government agency, the synagogue again has become the stunning edifice it once was. Opened in December 2007, the synagogue shows off its immense brass chandelier with its scores of glowing lights undimmed by original glass shades. Stained glass windows, 85 percent of which are original, let in rainbows of natural light. On special occasions, the beautifully carved wooden ark holds one of the twenty-four original Torahs found in the rubble of the building. The women's section upstairs is lit by crystal chandeliers, and on the western wall above it, is a colorful round rose window containing twelve Jewish stars, representing the twelve tribes of Israel. The synagogue is breathtaking.

The Museum at FIT

Location and Transit
227 West 27th Street
(212) 217-4558
fitnyc.edu/13666.asp
Subway: 1, A, C, E, F, N, R, M
Bus: M20, M23, M34

Hours and Admission
Tues.-Fri.	**12-8 p.m.**
Sat.	**10 a.m.-5 p.m.**
Sun.-Mon.	**Closed**
Free	

The Fashion Institute of Technology (FIT) is a premiere training school for those who plan to enter the world of fashion. The Museum at FIT, which was a wonderful surprise to us, is the only museum in New York City dedicated solely to the art of fashion. It has a permanent collection of more than fifty thousand garments and accessories to further its mission to advance education about fashion through various means. If you can't afford to shop at Henri Bendel or Madison Avenue couturiers, you can still have a great time at the Museum at FIT while immersing yourself in high fashion.

The day we visited, we saw two exhibits, both beautifully mounted and displayed. The first, *Night and Day*, was a historical overview of women's fashion as dictated by the mores of the period and the time of day. It presented women's clothing for formal and informal occasions, daywear and evening wear, from the eighteenth century to the present. In addition to the scores of magnificently clad mannequins in outfits, hats, shoes, and pocket books, the museum displayed beautiful and popular fabrics of the day framed on the walls behind the mannequins.

The second show, *American Beauty: Aesthetics and Innovation in Fashion,* explored innovative clothing construction in the United States. The exhibition showcased the daring, often groundbreaking work of American designers who focused primarily on the craft of dressmaking. The seventy-five looks on view were arranged according to their method of construction. These included the use of geometric forms, dressmaking, tailoring, construction, and embellishment. We saw the work of Claire McCardell, Halston, Charles James, Ralph Rucci, Jean Yu, Adrian, and Norman Norell, as well as others, equally talented but less known. We looked at these fabulous constructions called dresses and suits with wonder, appreciation, and avarice. We longed to take at least one home!

Unfortunately, the Museum at FIT does not have a shop or café, but there are plenty of restaurants nearby.

Museum of American Finance

Location and Transit

48 Wall Street
(212) 908-4110
moaf.org
Subway: 1, 2, 3, 4, 5, J, R, W
Bus: M1, M6, M9, M15

Hours and Admission

Tues.-Sat.	**10 a.m.-4 p.m.**
Sun.-Mon.	**Closed**
Adults	**$8**
Seniors and students	**$5**
Members and children	
under 6	**Free**

You can't get in to see the New York Stock Exchange to learn about stocks, bonds, and money in general, as it has been closed to visitors since 9/11. However, you can go to the Museum of American Finance, a Smithsonian affiliate, and learn more about the past, present, and future of the American economic system than you ever thought possible.

The Museum of American Finance is located on the corner of Wall and William Streets. It was once the site of three incarnations of the Bank of New York, the first bank in New York City. Founded by Alexander Hamilton, our first Secretary of the Treasury, the Bank of New York laid the cornerstone of its first building here in 1784.

The museum occupies thirty thousand square feet of space in the fully renovated 1929 Bank of New York building. The main exhibit space is located in the magnificent former banking hall on the Grand Mezzanine level. It features thirty-foot ceilings painted in two light colors to emphasize the architectural details, arched wall panels containing murals depicting aspects of commerce and banking, an elaborate marble staircase, pillars, and more.

Displaying some of the more than ten thousand financial documents and artifacts it owns, the museum seeks to describe the money, the power, and the history of the American financial system. The Financial Markets area deals with stocks, bonds, and commodities and includes intricately engraved financial certificates, a ticker tape that explains stock market symbols and figures, and videos of the New York Stock Exchange, the New York Mercantile Exchange, and Citigroup's bond trading floor. The Entrepreneurs section features interactive biographies of prominent business people.

Money: A History occupies a cave-like space meant to illicit the sensation of being in a large bank vault. It shows the history of American money, including beads, wampum, animal skins, and a bond issued to George Washington in 1792 featuring the first instance of the use of the dollar sign.

Also present are changing exhibits. We saw an interesting and amusing special exhibit called *Scandal: Financial Crime, Chicanery, and Corruption that Rocked America*, which covered the Teapot Dome scandal and Charles Ponzi, among others, and taught us that Bernie Madoff and Enron did not invent financial double dealing—although they certainly made a name for themselves doing it!

The museum has a small café and a gift shop where you can participate in the history of financial dealings that you just learned about.

The Museum of American Illustration

Location and Transit

128 East 63rd Street
(212) 838-2560
societyillustrators.org
Subway: 4, 5, 6, F
Bus: M98, M101, M102, M103, Q32

Hours and Admission

Tues.	10 a.m.-8 p.m.
Wed.-Fri.	10 a.m.-5 p.m.
Sat.	12-4 p.m.
Sun.-Mon.	Closed
Free	

Right around the corner from the China Institute is another small museum space with a decidedly different focus. The Society of Illustrators organizes this museum, with an exhibit space on two levels in order to fulfill its mission of supporting the art, history, and evolution of illustration in all of its forms.

Although a group of nine artists and one advising businessman founded the society in 1901, it only established its museum in 1981 with funds raised from its members and a large grant from the J. Walter Thompson Advertising Agency. The permanent collection includes hundreds of works by many of the greatest names in American painting and illustration, including Maxfield Parrish, N. C. Wyeth, Charles Dana Gibson, Frederic Remington, and Norman Rockwell. The collection is always expanding via purchases and donations, and portions of its extensive holdings are always on display.

We were delighted by the annual holiday show, held during the Christmas season, which features works by current members of the society. This is the only one of the society's exhibitions in which the paintings, prints, and photos are for sale. The society's scholarship program is partially financed by the proceeds of these sales. In May and June, the museum shows the works of the winners of the student scholarship competition program for the year. The competition is open to all college art majors and often receives more than 8,000 entries. Of these entries, only 125 are selected.

In October, visitors can see the 125 winners of the annual juried competition among children's book illustrators. The museum is the only venue in the country that highlights children's book illustration in this way. During that month, the museum hosts more than three hundred students on school visits. The young visitors can view the original art and read the books as well.

C. Leyendecker, cover of the Saturday ·ning Post, April 22, 1905. © The Saturday ·ning Post. (Courtesy Museum of American ·stration Purchase Fund)

Charles Dana Gibson, At the Recital. *Donated by C. D. Williams.* (Courtesy Museum of American Illustration)

Norman Rockwell, The Christmas Coach (Dover Coach), *December 28, 1935.* © The Saturday Evening Post. *Donated by the artist.* (Courtesy Museum of American Illustration)

Museum of Arts and Design

Location and Transit

2 Columbus Circle
(212) 299-7777
madmuseum.org
Subway: 1, A, B, C, D, F, N, Q, R, W
Bus: M5, M7, M10, M20, M30,
M104

Hours and Admission

Tues.-Wed., Sat.-Sun.	**11 a.m.-6 p.m.**
Thurs.-Fri.	**11 a.m.-9 p.m.**
Mon.	**Closed**
Adults	**$16**
Seniors	**$14**
Students	**$12**
Members and children 18 and under with ID	**Free**
Thurs. 6-9 p.m.	**Pay what you wish**

If you enjoy the unorthodox use of familiar materials, the imaginative use of unfamiliar materials, or simply the element of surprise, then the Museum of Arts and Design is for you.

Formerly named the American Craft Museum, the museum's mission is to collect, display, and interpret objects that document contemporary and historic innovation in craft, art, and design. When we entered the museum, we were greeted by introductions to the shows then on exhibit on upper floors. A giant white cloud of cut paper hung from the ceiling and bled onto the walls, almost mirroring the snow falling outside. A very large, brightly colored ceramic woman beckoned us to see her comrades upstairs.

The first upstairs exhibit was *Slash: Paper under the Knife*, which involved the use of paper and paper products in all kinds of interesting ways. Among the pieces was a huge statue of a mounted knight battling an enormous dragon beneath his horse's feet. The entire statue was made only of cardboard. Two portraits were delineated by shadows cast on a white wall by different size holes cut into black paper. *Bigger, Better, More* featured the ceramics and paintings of Viola Frey, a noted California artist. Frey was fascinated by the ceramic flea market statues and other finds she had collected all of her life and incorporated their color and sensibility into her art. *Portable Treasuries: Silver Jewelry from the Nadler Collection* drew us to cases of stunning, oversized silver jewelry, belts, and other objects created primarily in Asia.

In the galleries hang several interactive screens covered by small pictures of objects in its permanent collection, a kind of visual library. By simply touching an object on the screen, a visitor can enlarge the photo and learn about the object's composition and the artist who made it. One can also be directed to objects of a similar nature.

On the ninth floor and overlooking Central Park, the museum has a lovely restaurant, Roberto, which is privately operated. On the entry floor, it also has a wonderful gift shop full of beautiful, pricey objects for personal and home use.

Museum of Biblical Art

Location and Transit

1865 Broadway
(212) 408-1500
mobia.org
Subway: 1, A, B, C, D
Bus: M7, M11, M104

Hours and Admission

Tues.-Wed., Fri.-Sun.	10 a.m.-6 p.m.
Thurs.	10 a.m.-8 p.m.
Mon.	Closed
Free	

At home in a twenty-seven-hundred-square-foot exhibition space on the second floor of the American Bible Society headquarters, the Museum of Biblical Art is an independent entity. Despite its roots as a venue for temporary exhibitions by the Bible Society, particularly to showcase its vast collection of printed Bibles (second only to that of the Vatican), the Museum of Biblical Art now is a secular institution that exalts Bible-related art and its connections with both Jewish and Christian spirituality.

The design of the main exhibition space reflects the present nature of the museum as well as its history. It is a double-height room with single-height display walls subdividing it into smaller spaces. The exhibition space runs uninterrupted along the lower half of the back wall, but the upper portion of that wall is made of glass, allowing a visitor to see the society's archives with its rows of antique Bibles.

The light in the room was subdued but present enough to allow one to read the articles on the walls related to *Uneasy Communion: Jews, Christians, and the Altarpieces of Medieval Spain*. This exhibit reflected on the last two centuries in medieval Spain in the Kingdom of Aragon, the Kingdom of Valencia, and the region of Catalonia. At this time, according to documented evidence, there existed a cooperative relationship between Christians and Jews in the making of art both for the Church and the Jewish community. Jewish and Christian artists worked together in ateliers producing both *retablos* (large, multi-paneled altarpieces) as well as Latin and Hebrew manuscripts.

Former exhibitions have included *Reel Religion: A Century of Bible and Film, Scripture for the Eyes: Bible Illustration in Sixteenth Century Netherlandish Prints,* and *Tobi Kahn: Sacred Spaces of the Twenty-First Century,* which explored Kahn's liturgical and decorative works for the interior of Temple Emanu-El B'ne Jeshurun in Milwaukee, Wisconsin.

The museum also sponsors an extensive education program, which includes lectures and concerts related to the current exhibition.

Museum of Chinese in America

Location and Transit

215 Centre Street
(212) 619-4785
mocanyc.org
Subway: 6, J, N, R, Q, Z
Bus: M9, M15, M103

Hours and Admission

Tues.-Wed,	
Fri.-Sun.	**11 a.m.-6 p.m.**
Thurs.	**11 a.m.-9 p.m.**
Mon.	**Closed**
Adults	**$10**
Seniors with ID and students	
with ID	**$5**
Children under 12	**Free**

Designed by the architect Maya Lin, who gained prominence for her design of the Vietnam Memorial in Washington, DC, the present home of the Museum of Chinese in America is a small gem. Located between Chinatown and Soho in lower Manhattan, it was established in 1980 as the Chinatown History Project, which explored the traditions, struggles, and achievements of the Chinese in America. The site, converted from an industrial machine repair shop, now contains almost fourteen thousand square feet of beautifully designed exhibit space to house some of the sixty thousand documents and artifacts the museum owns. As Lao Tsu said, a journey of a thousand miles begins with a single step.

We saw the exhibit *With a Single Step: Stories in the Making of America*, which was both informative and unsettling. A room of documents and photographs described the early 1800s trade from the Far East, which brought luxury porcelains, eating implements, silks, and opium to America, along with many immigrants. On another wall, we saw scores of photos of prominent Chinese Americans, including Ah Bing, a farmer in Oregon who developed a new variety of cherry that bears his name; Dr. Faith Sai Leong, the first Chinese American female dentist; Chien Lung, known as the Chinese Potato King; Dong Kingman, a painter of the California School; and James Wong Howe, a cinematographer responsible for 130 films. The exhibit went on to outline the growing anti-Chinese sentiment that culminated in the 1882 Chinese Exclusion Act, passed by Congress and signed by Pres. Chester A. Arthur. Franklin Delano Roosevelt ended this law only after the attack on Pearl Harbor, probably because the United States would need all of its able-bodied men for the fighting forces. The exhibit also reviewed the American idea of Chinatown as mysterious, dark, and slightly wicked and the stereotypes with which early Hollywood represented the Chinese—consider Fu Manchu and the Dragon Lady.

Why have there been so many Chinese hand laundries in the United States? An exhibit entitled *The Eight-Pound Livelihood* explained the phenomenon. The Chinese were excluded from skilled trades. Preferring to be in business for themselves, they became hand launderers, and the irons that they used weighed eight pounds.

The museum also has a recreation of an original Chinatown shop as well as its own small gift shop. Outside its doors, there are Chinese restaurants galore. Museum personnel may give you advice on which to lunch in.

The Museum of Comic and Cartoon Art

Location and Transit
128 East 63rd Street
(212) 838-2560
moccany.com
Subway: 4, 5, 6, F
Bus: M98, M101, M102, M103, Q32

Hours and Admission

Tues.	**10 a.m.-8 pm.**
Wed.-Fri.	**10 a.m.-5 p.m.**
Sat.	**12-4 p.m.**
Sun.-Mon.	**Closed**
Free	

Upon entering the colorful three-room gallery of the Museum of Comic and Cartoon art, we were greeted by a large, painted portrait of Archie Andrews, the eternal teenager. There was also a class of youngsters obviously enjoying both time away from school and a visit to the museum.

The Museum of Comic and Cartoon Art was established to preserve, study, and display all genres of comic art, including animation, anime, cartoons, comic strips, gag cartoons, political illustrations, editorial cartoons, caricatures, and graphic novels, among many genres. It seeks to promote the understanding and appreciation of comic and cartoon art. Major exhibits change approximately every four months.

Archie was on prominent display because he and his gang were the subjects of the museum's major exhibition at that time, *The Art of Archie Comics*, which celebrated the sixty-five-plus years of this beloved family-friendly comic strip. Beginning in the 1960s and ending in the 2000s, the exhibit outlined, through cartoon strips, comic book covers, advertisements, and news stories, the evolution of Archie and his friends as they reflected the enormous changes in teenage life and attitudes during that period in American society.

In another room, the daredevil deeds of superheroes as they pursued villains were on display.

The museum holds classes in the various aspects of comic art for aspiring writers and illustrators. These classes are given by well-known cartoon experts. In the spring, the museum also sponsors the MoCCA Art Festival, which is held to appreciate the art of comics and attracts thousands of comic lovers and creators to a venue in New York City. Each year, the festival invites dozens of established and emerging creators, scholars, and other experts to participate in two days of lecture and discussion panels on a variety of comics and cartoon-related topics.

Courtesy Museum of Comic and Cartoon Art

Courtesy Museum of Comic and Cartoon Art

Museum of Jewish Heritage: A Living Memorial to the Holocaust

Location and Transit

36 Battery Place
(646) 437-4202
mjhnyc.org
Subway: 1, 4, 5, R
Bus: M5, M15, M20

Hours and Admission

Sun.-Tues., Thurs.	**10 a.m.-5:45 p.m.**
Wed.	**10 a.m.-8 p.m.**
Fri.	**10 a.m.-3 p.m.**
Sat.	**Closed**
Adults	**$12**
Seniors	**$10**
Students	**$7**
Members and children 12 and under	**Free**
Wed. 4-8 p.m.	**Free**

The Museum of Jewish Heritage is one of New York's most sophisticated ethnic museums. It is a must for Jewish tourists and natives as well as all others interested in twentieth-century Jewish history before, during, and after the Holocaust. It consists of two beautiful buildings on the waterfront facing New York Harbor and the Statue of Liberty.

The original six-sided building is meant to evoke the six million Jews who died during the Holocaust as well as the six-pointed Jewish symbol, the Star of David. This building holds the core exhibition space of the museum. More than twenty-five thousand artifacts are exhibited on three floors, each representing one aspect of the museum's three-fold story of Jewish life during the twentieth century: pre-war Jewish life, the war itself, and post-war renewal. All of the floors commemorate the voices of Jews from all walks of life, reflecting on their lives and trials. An audio tour of the museum featuring the voices of Meryl Streep and Itzhak Perlman is available in many languages and is a good way to go.

The museum also presents special exhibitions. Past special exhibitions have included *New York: City of Refuge, Stories from the Last Sixty Years* about Jewish immigration to New York City following the Holocaust and *Yahrzeit: September 11 Remembered,* which commemorated the September 11, 2001, terrorist attacks. We saw *Traces of Memory: A Contemporary Look at the Jewish Past in Poland,* a sensitive photo exhibit of the scarce remains of Jewish life in Poland.

The wonderful Keeping History Center of the museum is located in glass-walled room with panoramic views of New York Harbor and the Statue of Liberty. As a visitor walks around the room, stopping in designated carpeted circles and wearing ear phones, moving recordings of immigrants describing leaving their homeland, making the trip, their first impressions of their new country, and adapting to life in the United States play on the device.

We also visited the Garden of Stones, designed and installed by Andy Goldsworthy, as a space for contemplation, remembering those who perished in the Holocaust and honoring those who survived. In this garden, eighteen boulders form a series of narrow pathways in the space. A single dwarf oak sapling was planted in and rises from each boulder. The garden is an oasis of calm facing busy New York Harbor.

This museum has no eating location and discourages bringing food or drink onto the premises. It does have a lovely shop that sells books (both adult's and children's), DVDs, and all kinds of Judaica.

Museum of Sex

Location and Transit

233 5th Avenue
(212) 689-6337
museumofsex.com
Subway: 1, 6, R
Bus: M2, M3, M5, M6, M7

Hours and Admission

Sun.-Thurs.	**10 a.m.-8 p.m.**
Fri.-Sat.	**10 a.m.-9 p.m.**
Adults 18 and older	**$17.50 plus tax**
Seniors and students	**$15.25 plus tax**

You don't have to be a pervert to visit the Museum of Sex, but you do have to be more than eighteen years of age. Except for one gallery that featured a history of film pornography on many video screens in a darkened room, the museum offered a lot more education than arousal.

We saw two special exhibitions. One, *Rubbers: the Life and History*, was a fascinating display on the history of condoms. The exhibit described the use of condoms in Egypt and other early cultures and traced the beginnings of the modern-day prophylactic and from what they were made. We learned that one of the first manufacturers of condoms in the United States had been a butcher and gotten the idea of using treated casings from animal intestines. That butcher later became the founder of a condom company. The exhibit featured an entire wall of names for condoms from "anti-baby" to "zucchini beanie." The exhibit also included a series of showcases on syphilis and other sexually transmitted diseases, which condoms help to prevent. There was also interesting art based on the condom by Randy Polumbo, Masami Teraoka, and Keith Haring, whose subject largely was AIDS awareness.

The second special exhibition was also an eye opener. Called the *Sex Lives of Animals*, this, too, offered information not often discussed. In an introductory passage the museum stated that it hoped to investigate sexual behavior in the animal kingdom and provoke interrogation of human misconceptions. Much of this exhibit was based upon the research of scientists in the field, watching and recording the behavior of the animals they had chosen to study. One interesting result of this work was the finding that same-sex relationships exist in more than five hundred animal species and that females take on male character traits in several other species.

The museum's shop is available to visitors without gallery admission. There, you will find all kinds of books, puzzles, t-shirts, stationery, and other merchandise—all with a sexual twist, and a good deal of it quite funny.

Museum of the City of New York

Location and Transit
1220 5th Avenue
(212) 534-1672
mcny.org
Subway: 2, 3, 6
Bus: M1, M2, M3, M4, M106

Hours and Admission

Sun.-Sat.	10 a.m.-6 p.m.
Adults	$10
Seniors and students	$6
Families	$20
Members and children under 12	Free

Originally located in Gracie Mansion, the official home of the New York City mayor, the museum was founded in 1923. It moved to its present location, a gracious Fifth Avenue mansion built expressly as a repository for its extensive materials about New York as a historic, artistic, and cultural legacy.

The first floor showcases its special exhibitions, which change from eight to ten times per year and usually remain on display for three to six months each. We saw an exhibit about the life and work of Eero Saarinen, which included his mother's painting of him as a child as well as a display of the famous chairs that made him a household name.

On the second floor, begin your tour with a wonderful video called *Timescapes: A Multi-Media Portrait of New York*, which provides an overview of the development of New York City from its Dutch beginnings to the present. Time periods include the colonial city from 1609 to 1783, the first waves of European immigration from 1825 to 1865, the growing metropolis of 1865 to 1900, the modern city from 1900 to 1920, the cosmopolitan city from 1920 to 1945, and the economic, political, and cultural renaissance of 1975 through 2001.

The museum's vast holdings include more than a half million pieces, including paintings, photographs, toys, costumes, rare books, manuscripts, and sculptures. It also holds the finest and most complete collection of Currier and Ives hand-colored lithographs. A world-renowned collection on American theater, including set design, costume renderings, original scripts, posters, and props reside here as well.

The museum offers a year-round calendar of special events, presentations, and educational programs for both adults and children. In addition, there is a small shop and a café featuring local New York-based products.

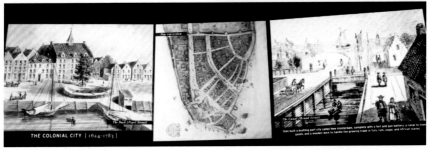

National Academy Museum

Location and Transit

1083 5th Ave
(212) 369-4880
nationalacademy.org
Subway: 4,5,6
Bus: M1, M2, M3, M4

Hours and Admission

Wed.-Sun.	**11 a.m.-6 p.m.**
Mon.-Tues.	**Closed**
Adults	**$15**
Seniors and students with ID	**$10**
Members and children under 12	**Free**

On the famous Museum Mile across the street from the Whitney Museum, the National Academy Museum is a veritable gem. Housed in a historic Beaux-Arts mansion formerly owned by philanthropist Archer Milton Huntington and his wife, sculptor Anna Hyatt Huntington, it provides a gracious home for seeing the art it owns and exhibits. The National Academy has a collection of more than seven thousand works of American art, one of the largest such collections in the country. Since its beginnings in 1825, it has amassed works from the nineteenth century through the present, including works from the Hudson River School and the American Impressionist and the Abstract Expressionist movements. In addition to amassing American art, the National Academy has two other services. It is an honorary association of professional artists, known as Academicians, elected to membership by their peers, and it offers a full range of art classes to serious students of all ages.

It was our good fortune to happen upon the *185th Invitational Exhibition of Contemporary American Art* chosen by artists and available to the public. This eclectic exhibit featured sixty-five emerging and established artists chosen by a jury of National Academicians. Some of the works were puzzling, others were thought provoking, and some others elicited very positive or negative reactions, but all engendered a deeper understanding of the directions that contemporary art is taking. Particularly interesting was a video installation by Nina Yankowitz, *Buried Treasures/Secrets in the Sciences*, which told the story of female scientists and their history, and a very large cut-paper piece hanging in the entrance hallway by Anna Lambrini Moisadis.

The house has a wonderful winding wrought-iron staircase in which small oval portraits of the Academy members are embedded. Looking up through the floors, one can see, on the topmost ceiling, the mechanism that Anna Hyatt Huntington used to lift and lower her sculptures, one of which, *Diana*, graces the rotunda of the museum.

This museum has no eating establishment, but its shop offers an eclectic array of wonderful objects to take home and enjoy.

The National Jazz Museum in Harlem

Location and Transit

104 East 126th Street, 2D
(212) 348-8300
jazzmuseuminharlem.org
Subway: 2, 3, 4, 5, 6
Bus: M125

Hours and Admission

Mon.-Fri.	10 a.m.-4 p.m.
Sat.-Sun.	Closed

Donations welcome

For those people who love jazz, visiting the National Jazz Museum in Harlem is a must. There, while you look around the one-room gallery, you can hear your favorite jazz music by simply picking out a CD or two from the large catalogue of CD covers and asking the volunteer in charge to play it.

The museum was founded in 1996 by Leonard Garment, Art D'Lugoff, and David Levy. Garment, a former presidential adviser, played the saxophone with Woody Herman for a brief period.

When we visited, the museum featured the work of Hank O'Neal, renowned photographer, who documented much of Harlem's jazz past and some of its present. There were wonderful studies of Eubie Blake, Milt Hinton, Dizzy Gillespie, Joe Williams, and a score of other well-known musicians of the jazz canon. One interesting artistic piece that is part of the museum's permanent exhibit is chess set created by Arthur Payn in which all of the pieces consist of musicians playing a variety of instruments.

Since the exhibit space is small, a visitor might just wish to sit on one of two comfortable leather sofas and simply listen to his or her favorite jazz music while thumbing through current jazz magazines or one of the many books in the library. A guest also might choose to stay for one of the evening educational events, since education is part of the museum's core mission. Events range from discussing jazz for casual listeners, the influence of the Harlem neighborhood, or features on specific musicians.

All in all, the National Jazz Museum in Harlem is a terrific place to visit if you love jazz or would like to know more about it. As an added bonus, there are wonderful places to eat nearby in Harlem.

The National Museum of the American Indian—New York

Location and Transit

1 Bowling Green
(212) 514-3700
americanindian.si.edu
Subway: 1, 4, 5, J, R, Z
Bus: M5, M15, M20

Hours and Admission

Mon.-Sun.	10 a.m.-5 p.m.
Thurs.	10 a.m.-8 p.m.
Free	

The branch of the National Museum of the American Indian in downtown Manhattan, also known as the George Gustav Heye Center, is part of the complex of the Smithsonian Institution's fifteen museums and one of three sites that comprise the National Museum of the American Indian. It is devoted to exploring and celebrating the culture, art, and history of the all the native peoples in the Western Hemisphere through special exhibits that reflect upon and educate about these early societies.

The Heye Center is located within a landmark building, the Alexander Hamilton US Custom House, which is an added bonus of visiting the museum. It is a remarkable and fine example of Beaux-Arts architecture and extensive indoor marble-clad spaces.

We saw *A Song for the Horse Nation*, an exhibit that shed light on the relationship between native communities and their horses. In the fifteenth century, Christopher Columbus introduced horses into the New World and changed native life forever. Before the introduction of horses, the hunting for food and making clothing, for example, was incredibly time intensive, leaving no space for much else. However, their lives dramatically changed when they embraced the horse. With horses, tribes could move farther and faster with larger loads and hunt more effectively. Horses gave native communities more time to devote to art, spirituality, and philosophy. A Teton Sioux song contextualized a picture indelibly stamped in American minds—one of Native peoples and their horses: "Out of the earth/ I sing for them,/ A Horse nation/ I sing for them."

The museum curates traveling exhibitions, produces publications, and also features public programs, including performances and lectures highlighting various aspects the Americas' native peoples. However, it is too bad that the Smithsonian does not do more with this incredible space.

Neue Galerie

Location and Transit

1048 Fifth Avenue
(212) 628-6200
neuegalerie.org
Subway: 4, 5, 6, B, C
Bus: M1, M2, M3, M4, M86

Hours and Admission

Thurs.-Mon.	**11 a.m.-6 p.m.**
Tues.-Wed.	**Closed**
Adults	**$20**
Seniors and students with ID	**$10**
Children under 12	**Not admitted**

If you enjoy the works of Gustav Klimt, then the Neue Galerie is a must-see on your list. Housed in a Beaux-Arts building on Museum Mile, the Galerie exhibits the best of Austrian and German early twentieth-century art and design. It is the result of the dedication, vision, and friendship between two men, art dealer Serge Sabarsky and philanthropist and collector Ronald S. Lauder.

At various times, the Neue Galerie exhibits the works of Gustav Klimt, Egon Schiele, Oskar Kokoschka, Vasily Kandinsky, Paul Klee, Franz Marc, Lyonel Feininger, László Moholy-Nagy, and more.

A marvelous exhibit called *Franz Xaver Messerschmidt, 1736-1783: From Neo-Classicism to Expressionism, The Sculpture of Franz Haver Messerschmidt* introduced us to the surprisingly talented and tortured artist. To us, children during World War II, the word *Messerschmidt* meant only one thing—a small but dangerous enemy German fighter plane. It was our surprise to meet, at the Neue Galerie, a very different Messerschmidt. Messerschmidt trained as a classically baroque sculptor with many significant early successes. However, a turn of events brought his talent to a darker place. In the last years of his short life, he created sixty-nine character heads, all of which have distorted features and many of which were portraits of the artist with a fiercely grimacing mien. The heads are remarkable and mesmerizing. The curators of this exhibit explain that this sculptor preceded the expressionist movement by more than a century. The museum exhibited these dramatic heads in rooms delicately stenciled in the style of an eighteenth-century salon.

We also saw *Postcards of the Wiener Werkstätte: Selections from the Leonard A. Lauder Collection.* These beautiful, colorful small rectangles were the work of fifty-seven known artists affiliated with the renowned workshop and gallery. Although created as postcards, they now are considered original prints that document events of the era, celebrate holidays, depict fashions and accessories, and illustrate places in Vienna and Europe. Some of the cards are humorous or include popular sayings of the period.

The gallery has a wonderful book store and a beautiful—albeit pricey—shop. The Café Sabarsky is a lovely upscale dining establishment. Elevators are available.

Courtesy Neue Galerie

Courtesy Neue Galerie

New Museum

Location and Transit
235 Bowery
(212) 219-2222
newmuseum.org
Subway: 6, D, F, N, R
Bus: M6, M103

Hours and Admission

Wed., Fri.-Sun.	11 a.m.-6 p.m.
Thurs.	11 a.m.-9 p.m.
Mon.-Tues.	Closed
Adults $14	
Seniors $12	
Students $10	
Members and children under 18	Free

The New Museum is a pleasure to enter. The entrance is large and light-filled, holding the check-in counter, the cloak room, the shop, and the café. It values its space and maximizes it to the utmost. The New Museum was the first museum founded in New York City devoted exclusively to contemporary art post-World War II. It was founded humbly in 1977 in a one-room office on Hudson Street by curator Marcia Tucker, who wanted to give living artists the opportunity to exhibit their work and provide the interested public with knowledge of them. In 2007, the New Museum opened its own building in a former parking lot with an innovative design by the architects Kazuyo Sejima + Ryue Nishizawa/SANAA. The building was conceived as a stack of rectilinear boxes shifted off-axis around a central steel core. The exterior is clad in a shimmering anodized aluminum skin, and the interior is marked by three column-free gallery floors of different ceiling heights and skylights that flood the spaces with light.

To truly appreciate the New Museum, a viewer must leave prescribed concepts about art at the door. On the day we visited, one long wall that contained the elevators was covered by a dramatic black and white mural by assume vivid astro focus (AVAF), part of the major exhibition *Skin Fruit: Selections from the Dakis Joannou Collection.* The exhibit was curated by the iconoclastic artist Jeff Koons. As it was for us, many pieces will delight, others, bewilder, and some, evoke hostility or misunderstanding. For example, Tino Sehgal's work *This is Propaganda* consisted of nine white body bags laid side by side on a grey floor while a museum guard repeatedly sang "This is propaganda/you know/you know" in a fine contralto. One left the space ruminating on the meanings of the work.

If you go to the New Museum, you may not like what you see. You may not understand what you see. You may be enchanted by what you see. But you certainly will not be bored. In addition, the small café is a definite win. It is separated from the gallery by a glass wall that encourages visitors to examine the art while they dine.

New York City Fire Museum

Location and Transit

278 Spring Street
(212) 691-1303
nycfiremuseum.org
Subway: 1, C, E
Bus: M10, M21

Hours and Admission

Sun.-Sat.	10 a.m.-5 p.m.
Adults	$8
Seniors, students with a valid ID, and children 12 and under	$5

There were fire engines everywhere—shiny, red, with gleaming brass accents, all in pristine condition. There was a horse-drawn chief's buggy from 1892, a metropolitan steamer from 1912, a hand pumper from 1790, and a horse-drawn steam engine from 1901—and that was only the ground floor of this two-level museum. I had to do all I could from keeping my comrade honest; he wanted to climb onto the engines, even though he knew that doing so was prohibited.

On the second floor were the prides of the New York City Fire Museum. We saw a veteran pumper from 1840 with a double-decker engine that took more than forty-eight men to pull and operate. It starred in the parade at the unveiling of the Statue of Liberty in 1886. We saw a Hingham pumper from 1855 and the Steinway Hose Company No. 7 with a hand-drawn hose reel dating from 1875. There was even a weather vane showing a horse drawn fire wagon.

There were other riches in this museum housed in a former Engine Company No. 30 fire house dating from 1905. We saw a wall of patches collected from various fire departments, medals denoting decades of valor, a mannequin fully suited as a fireman, fire jackets in various sizes that a visitor could try on, and an area devoted to fire dogs.

The museum also devoted one room to September 11, 2001, the grim day that saw the loss of 343 brave firefighters. The memorial consisted of a tripartite construction faced with tiles containing the photos, ranks, and companies of the heroic men.

In addition to the engines, the second floor held a plethora of memorabilia, including drawings and prints depicting the national firefighting life. There were photos, scrolls, tapestries, and Currier and Ives prints (Currier served as a NYC volunteer fireman during the 1850s). An exhibit of helmets showed the felt top-hat helmets used early in Philadelphia as well as the New York City helmet made of leather. Its original shape is still used today.

There is a small shop selling firefighting books, t-shirts, and souvenirs. The museum is a great place for families and offers much to excite and enthrall children of all ages.

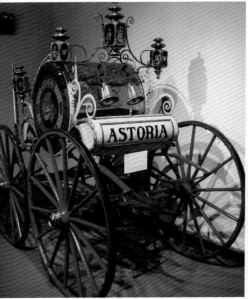

The New York City Police Museum

Location and Transit
100 Old Slip
(212) 480-3100
nycpolicemuseum.org
Subway: 1, 2, 3, 4, 5, R, W
Bus: M9, M15

Hours and Admission

Mon.-Sat.	**10 a.m.-5 p.m.**
Sun.	**12-5 p.m.**
Adults	**$8**
Seniors, students, and children	**$5**
Children under 2	**Free**

The New York City Police Museum is located in an impressive Italianate former mansion near the lower Manhattan waterfront. In an early incarnation, it housed the New York City Police Precinct No. 1, the eight-member force that first protected the young Dutch colony by carrying green lanterns and rattles. Whistles arrived later, but the green lanterns survive to this day as beacons in front of all of New York's police precincts. The original eight police officers are commemorated in the Tiffany 1876 design of the first police shield, which bears an eight-pointed star. The copper shield gave a familiar nickname to the men who wore it, subsequently known as "coppers."

It is a fun place to visit, especially with children. Lots of smiling youngsters, proudly wearing their Junior Police badges, were leaving the building when we entered. For adults, the history of the department is fascinating, as is the extensive collection of firearms, the reconstructed jail cell, and the opportunity for your own mug shot to be taken. A visiting exhibit, *The Life and Legacy of Lieutenant Petrosino*, was an interesting introduction into Italian crime committed in the late nineteenth and early twentieth centuries in New York and how the police handled it. Petrosino was the chief expert on Italian crime and a crusader against the Black Hand thugs. He died at the hands of the Mafia in Palermo, Italy.

The important exhibit outlining the changes to the police department following the events of September 11, 2001, is a must for every New Yorker and visitor to the city. In a video in that exhibit, Mayor Michael Blumberg conjectures that New York City will continue to be a target for terrorism but that terrorists will not succeed as they did in 2001 because the police are more prepared. Now, the city has one thousand officers specifically dedicated to counter-terrorism, critical response vehicles, an Intelligence Division that seeks to uncover possible terror planning using the Internet, and Hercules Teams, officers specially equipped and trained to defuse bombs and other tools of terrorism. In addition, police now hold surges, assemblies at various points across the city to practice swift gatherings over a large territory. A particularly unsettling but dramatic exhibition was *Policing a Changed City*, a long wall recounting the many terror attacks on New York City during the last decades. On the same floor, one could revisit videos and other materials recounting the September 2001 attacks.

New-York Historical Society Museum and Library

Location and Transit

170 Central Park West
(212) 873-3400
nyhistory.org
Subway: 1, B, C
Bus: M10, M79

Hours and Admission

Tues.-Thurs., Sat.	**10 a.m.-6 p.m.**
Fri.	**10 a.m.-8 p.m.**
Sun.	**11 a.m.-5 p.m.**
Mon.	**Closed**
Adults	**$15**
Seniors, educators, and active military	**$12**
Students	**$10**
Children (5-13)	**$5**
Children 4 and under	**Free**

The first time we visited the New-York Historical Society Museum and Library on Central Park West, the oldest museum in New York City, it was surrounded by barricades and ditches. The museum was in the process of renovation, so we disconsolately went away. When we returned in November 2011, we were greeted by men and women in historical outfits, the men wearing Revolutionary War-era colonial officer's uniforms and the women dressed in long calico skirts and aprons and bearing baskets.

Entering the entirely refurbished space, we were delighted by the extraordinary changes that make this museum a must on any visitor's or native's list. In the white and marble lobby is a large painting that turns out to be a twelve-screen video installation in which a little dog and a large crowd pulling down the statue of King George all move with accompanying sound. Small children were enchanted by the movement in the "painting," and many adults were as well.

Inside the beautiful lobby space was part of an exhibit called *Revolution!: The Atlantic World Reborn*, which sought to explore the connections among the American, French, and Haitian revolutions. *Liberty, Liberté*, was filled with paintings, statues, and objects from the three wars. Interesting and creative touches that we admired were the wall signage that identified the object with a tiny picture so that there would be no mistake about its description and small, circular glass-covered caches in the marble floor containing artifacts excavated after the American Revolution.

The museum offers an eighteen-minute colorful multimedia film about the history of New York in a comfortable and expansive auditorium.

The fourth floor of the museum exhibits some of the many objects it holds in its permanent collection. Called the Henry Luce Center for Study of American Culture, this center had hundreds of chairs, tables, and paintings on display. We were astonished by the 132 beautifully lit and colorful examples of Tiffany lamps and other glass works. The Robert Lehman Gallery of American Sculpture held a large bust of Abraham Lincoln as well as one of Ernie Pyle. The myriads of sculptures on view are only a small part of the museum's collection. I was drawn to the many landscapes of New York that traced the physical evolution of my city.

This museum has much more to offer a visitor, including the Dimenna Children's History Museum and the Barbara K. Lipman Children's History Library, which were designed especially to engage young visitors in interactive experiences. There is an extensive shop that is available without having to pay for admission. There is also a restaurant on the main floor, Caffè Storico. The museum is not really small; it would be difficult to see it all in one visit, much like the Frick or the Museum of Art and Design. However, we recorded our visit because it is, well, not the Met.

9/11 Tribute Center

Location and Transit

120 Liberty St
(212) 393-9160 x. 138
tributewtc.org
Subway: 2, 3, 4, 5, A, C, E, J, R, Z
Bus: M1, M6

Hours and Admission

Mon.-Sat.	**10 a.m.-6 p.m.**
Sun.	**10 a.m.-5 p.m.**

Last tickets sold half-hour before closing

Adult	**$17 (Gallery only)**
Seniors, students, and military	**$12 (Gallery only)**
Children ages 6-12	**$5 (Gallery only)**

The 9/11 Tribute Center is without doubt one of the most difficult exhibits to visit. Because we are native New Yorkers, it forced us to remember and contemplate that awful day in 2001. Definitely bring your tissue box for this experience—we were surrounded by many tearful visitors and we cried ourselves.

The exhibit begins with a film exploring the development of the World Trade Center, which at the time was the largest architectural project since the building of the pyramids in Egypt. A street map of lower Manhattan covered the floor on which we stood. This section of the exhibit bore the ironic name *Peace and Stability through Trade.*

In subsequent spaces, the tribute began in earnest with a film of the attack and its aftermath. In one glass case, we saw a window retrieved from one of the attacking planes. In another there were haunting reminders of the many victims: shoes, cell phones, and the caps of men and women in uniform. These were found in the mass of rubble created by the collapse of the two giant buildings. Another section, perhaps the most difficult to experience, was a video simply listing the name of each of the hundreds of victims. The video took four hours to complete. On three surrounding walls, we saw photos of the men and women who died that day. It was called the Wall of Hope.

A staircase festooned with lengths of small colorful cranes, a Japanese symbol of peace, led to the lower floor. On the lower floor were hundreds of cards written by visitors on the subject "9/11 teaches . . ." Visitors were encouraged to fill these cards out and add their testimony to others. The resulting compilation of moving stories explained how the lives of survivors and others have changed as a result of that devastating day.

Certainly, a visit to this memorable exhibit will remind you once again about the sanctity of life and Americans' unity and strength in overcoming obstacles.

Onassis Cultural Center

Location and Transit

645 5th Avenue
(212) 486-4448
onassisusa.org
Subway: 6, B, D, E, F, M
Bus: M1, M2, M3, M4, M5, Q32

Hours and Admission

Mon.-Sat.	**10 a.m.-6 p.m.**
Sun.	**Closed**
Free	

The Onassis Cultural Center is part of the Alexander S. Onassis Public Benefit Foundation (USA). This small but elegant museum occupies part of the ground level floor of the midtown Olympic Tower. The museum and the foundation were established to disseminate Hellenic culture throughout the United States. The foundation sponsors art exhibits; theater, dance, and musical performances; poetry readings; and lectures, all of which are free to the public.

Heroes: Mortals and Myths in Ancient Greece was the uplifting exhibit we saw one rainy, dark day. It sought to define what makes someone a hero or a heroine. The heroes of ancient Greece have become to us the matter of myth, but to the Greeks of ancient times they were not fictional at all. They were real men and women who showed bravery and virtue during their lives and transcended death. Belief in their post-mortem supernatural powers led to their worship through ritual, offerings, and art. The exhibit examined the lives of four major Greek heroes, Odysseus, Helen, Achilles, and Herakles, through some of the original art created in their honor. Among the beautiful and strange objects we saw was a small bronze statue from the fourth century BC, which showed one of Odysseus's men transformed into a pig—you may remember this incident from reading *The Odyssey*. A carved stone relief depicted the sirens, beautiful singing women who drove sailors mad and sank their ships but whom Odysseus cleverly outsmarted. One container depicted Achilles and Ajax playing a board game during a lull in the Trojan War with their trusty weapons on the floor beside them should they need them in a hurry. One amphora depicted Herakles completing his twelve labors. A beautiful first century BC bronze statue was of Herakles as an old man. Much of the artwork appeared on red clay pots of many sizes with beautifully detailed scenes in either black or white. The museum also featured fine votive reliefs made of marble.

This easily accessible museum in the midst of New York City may well whet your appetite for a Greek adventure—but this is certainly easier to get to.

The Paley Center for Media

Location and Transit

25 West 52nd Street
(212) 621-6600
paleycenter.org
Subway: B, D, E, F, M, N, R
Bus: M1, M2, M3, M4, M5, M6, M7

Hours and Admission

Wed.-Sun.	**12-6 p.m.**
Thurs.	**12-8 p.m.**
Mon.-Tues.	**Closed**
Adults	**$10**
Seniors and students	**$8**
Children under 14	**$5**

Originally known as the Museum for Broadcasting and then the Museum for Television and Radio, the Paley Center is not a museum in the standard sense. Instead of paintings and artifacts, the Paley Center collects and makes available almost 150,000 television and radio programs and has locations in both New York City and Los Angeles. Founded by William S. Paley, the chief executive and founder of CBS, the New York City Paley Center is located in a beautiful marble space designed by the famed architect Philip Johnson. This institution is a television lover's Eden.

The large and impressive entry hall holds the reception desk and the Spielberg Gallery, a space for changing exhibitions, special events, and fundraisers. We saw magnificent, oversized color photographs by Timothy Greenfield Sanders of major media personalities, including charming portraits of Whoopi Goldberg and Lee Daniels, the director of *Precious.*

The center's mission is to promote conversation about television, radio, and other media in professional, public, cultural, and creative arenas. To do this, it provides a library, where a visitor can choose a program from the collection and watch and/or listen to it on an individual console or as part of a group of four on a family console.

Two theaters provide comfortable spaces for viewing special

presentations. We saw the hilarious pilot episode of *Seinfeld*, which originally aired on July 5, 1989. In addition to Jerry, the pilot included George and Kramer, all much younger versions of the gang we have come to know and love. We also saw Funny Women of Television, which featured the work of many well-known comediennes, including Lucille Ball, Carol Burnett, Mary Tyler Moore, Candice Bergen, and Tracey Ullman.

Elevators provide easy access to the theaters and the library. The first floor also offers a gift shop that provides videos, recordings, and books. There is no restaurant, but the Paley Center is a wonderful Midtown venue for a fun hour or two of entertainment and rest. If you love television, you may not ever want to leave.

Courtesy Paley Center for Media

Rose Museum at Carnegie Hall

Location and Transit

154 West 57th Street, 2nd Floor
(212) 247-7800
carnegiehall.org
Subway: 1, A, B, C, D, E, F, N, Q, R
Bus: M5, M7, M10, M20, M31,
** M57, M104**

Hours and Admission

Sun.-Sat.	**11 a.m.-4:30 p.m.**
July 1-September 14	**Closed**
Free	

Music lovers will find a small enchanted haven on the second floor of Carnegie Hall. The space, which opened in 1991, is replete with large photographs of the renowned performers and conductors who have filled the famous hall beneath with music. In addition, cases hold a century's worth of programs, which serve to reconstruct the history of the world-famous concert hall. The museum's permanent collection also includes record covers, one of Benny Goodman's clarinets, Judy Garland's sequined jacket, a ring owned by Beethoven, and a pair of Johannes Brahms's eyeglasses.

The museum hosts exhibits for special occasions. Past exhibits featured Marian Anderson, the first African American to sing at the Metropolitan Opera; George and Ira Gershwin (held in honor of George's one hundredth birthday); and Leonard Bernstein.

Although the establishment of Lincoln Center endangered the future of Carnegie Hall, Isaac Stern spearheaded a campaign to save the structure and its contents. At that time, in 1960, the City of New York purchased the hall, and it became a National Historic Landmark in 1962.

Adjacent to the museum is a small museum store that sells musical artifacts, children's toy musical instruments, and CDs.

The Rubin Museum of Art

Location and Transit
150 West 17th Street
(212) 620-5000
rmanyc.org
Subway: 1, 2, 3, 4, 5, 6, A, C, E, F,
    L, M, N, Q, R, V, W
Bus: B20, M5, M6, M7, M20

Hours and Admission

Mon., Thurs.	11 a.m.-5 p.m.
Wed.	11 a.m.-7 p.m.
Fri.	11 a.m.-10 p.m.
Sat.-Sun.	11 a.m.-6 p.m.
Tues.	Closed
Adults	$10
Seniors and students	$5
Members and children 12 and under	Free
Fri. 6-10 p.m.	Free

Years ago, Donald and Shelley Rubin spent half their $3,000 savings on a Tibetan painting, an event that began their lifelong love affair with Asian art. Donald went on to become a wealthy man, and the couple continued to learn about and buy art from the Asian continent.

Since its opening in October 2004, the Rubin Museum has been recognized as the premiere museum of Himalayan art in the western world. Originally displayed in Mr. Rubin's office, the collection now resides in a gracious building, formerly occupied by Barney's Boys Town. Its beautiful, six-story spiral staircase, which echoed the spirit of the mandala, convinced Mr. Rubin that this was the perfect place for his museum.

Now a non-profit organization, the museum mounts changing shows arranged from its nearly twenty-five-hundred-piece permanent collection as well as loans from around the world. It takes great pains to show off these priceless artifacts in a hushed, colorful, and peaceful environment that reflects the spiritual genesis of the works.

We saw *Mandala: the Perfect Circle*, which took the visitor on a voyage of this central Buddhist artistic representation of man and the universe from the eighth to the twenty-first century, displaying some of the oldest and most colorful known mandalas in the world. On exhibit was also *Victorious Ones: Jain Images of Perfection*, which showed artistic representations of the Jinas, the founding figures of Jainism. We also skimmed through the *Red Book*, by Carl Jung, a large, illuminated volume illustrating his ideas on the unconscious and his fascination with the mandala.

We were lucky to be accompanied by Juliette, a guide who has been with the museum since its inception and whose knowledge and enthusiasm about the works and the religions is remarkable. There is also a shop featuring items related to current exhibitions and a café offering a cultural dining experience.

Salmagundi Art Club

Location and Transit
47 5th Avenue
(212) 255-7740
salmagundi.org
Subway: 4, 5, 6, F, L, M, N, Q, R
Bus: M1, M2, M3, M5

Hours and Admission

Mon.-Fri.	1-6 p.m.
Sat.-Sun.	1-5 p.m.
Free	

The Salmagundi Art Club was founded in New York City in 1871 and is one of the oldest art organizations in the United States. It began when a small group of professional artists met on Saturday evenings in the studio of J. Scott Hartley, a famous sculptor and the son-in-law of George Inness. There, they critiqued one another's work, painted, sketched, and enjoyed themselves among their peers. In 1917, the club bought a lovely Fifth Avenue brownstone—still its permanent home—and became the center of artistic activity in Greenwich Village for many years. Its roster of members and former members composes the history of American art since the nineteenth century.

In reality, while it mounts a variety of exhibitions and owns a good deal of art, the Salmagundi Club is not a museum, as much of the art displayed is for sale. However, it is a good place to see what contemporary artists are doing.

The day we visited, the club was showing the *Annual Black and White Exhibition*, which, true to its name, was comprised of works done only in black and white. Among the many pieces lining the walls of the large exhibit space were photographs; pen and ink drawings; oil, acrylic, and water color paintings; pencil works; etchings; monotypes; and charcoal drawings. It was remarkable what emotional heft those two colors were able to accomplish.

Paper Makers Hands, a photograph of a worn workman's hands, by Kate Faust, was particularly compelling, as was a graphic by Tadeusz Parzygnat called *A Winter*. In this work the artist combined tiers of raw-looking wood and paint to create a chilling scene of frozen winter. These two works were winners of major awards given by the jury.

A stop at the Salmagundi Club if you are downtown can be very rewarding, if you are interested in contemporary art with the spirit of community and communication among current artists. You never know what you may find.

Scandinavia House

Location and Transit

58 Park Avenue
(212) 779-3587
scandinaviahouse.org
Subway: 4, 5, 6, 7, S
Bus: M1, M2, M3, M4, M5

Hours and Admission

Tues.-Sat.	**12-6 p.m.**
Sun.-Mon.	**Closed**
Admission varies by exhibition	

Scandinavia House, the Nordic Center in America, is not really a museum. It is actually the home of the American-Scandinavian Foundation, a non-profit organization committed to promoting educational, cultural, and professional exchanges between the United States and the Nordic countries: Denmark, Finland, Iceland, Norway, and Sweden. The foundation offers fellowships, cultural grants, traineeships, publications, films, exhibitions, and other public programs.

When you first enter Scandinavia House, you find a small hallway that leads to a lovely restaurant, Smörgås Chef, one of three restaurants of the same name in New York City. The all-white restaurant, surrounded by a white fence, with trees in the middle of tables, offers a very Scandinavian menu at a modest price. It is a great place to rest and revive when you are visiting museums in the area.

Also on the main floor is a wonderful shop offering items from Scandinavia, including well-designed silver jewelry, beautiful Nordic wool sweaters, colorful children's books, Swedish glass, and stainless steel.

The second floor contains the exhibition space that, in the past, has featured exhibits such as *Garbo's Garbos: Portraits from Her Private Collection, Five Centuries of Swedish Silver: Treasures from the Rohsska Museum, Trolls and Billy Goats: Norwegian Fairy Tales and Legends,* and *From Wood to Architecture: Recent Designs from Finland.* When we were there, we saw *Snøhetta: Architecture—Landscape—Interior,* which afforded insight into the design mind of the award-winning and environmentally conscious architectural firm responsible for the Bibliotheca in Alexandria, Egypt; the Norwegian National Opera and Ballet in Oslo, Norway; and the planned National September 11 Memorial Museum Pavilion in New York.

Our visit was satisfying on all counts—we ate in the charming restaurant and bought several objects from the shop.

The Schomburg Center for Research in Black Culture

Location and Transit
515 Malcolm X Boulevard
(212) 491-2200
nypl.org/locations/schomburg
Subway: 2, 3
Bus: M7, M102

Hours and Admission
Mon., Fri.-Sat.	**10 a.m.-6 p.m.**
Tues.-Thurs.	**12-8 p.m.**
Sun.	**Closed**
Free	

The Schomburg Center in Harlem is not really a museum. It is, in fact, a branch of the New York Public Library—and an interesting branch at that. It holds exhibits relating to its central research and is definitely worth a visit, particularly if one is far uptown.

As we walked into the glass-fronted building, we were astonished by an extensive exhibit called *Soulful Stitching: Patchwork Quilts by Africans (Siddis) of India.* What a dynamic and eye-filling exhibit this turned out to be! The vast majority of these astonishing quilts are made by an adult female family member, who creates these beautiful items for the family's use. The quilts on view, measured in hands (the length between the elbow and fingertip of the quilter), were fashioned primarily by the Siddi Women's Cooperative. One particularly eye-catching piece was titled *An American Spirit to Ride Anywhere from Utah to Oregon*, an unusual name for an unusual artwork.

In the formal exhibit space upstairs, an interesting photography show called *Harlem Views/ Diasporan Visions: The New Harlem Renaissance* caught our attention. These were studies by photographers such as Beverly Terry, Karl Crutchfield, Kwame Brathwaite, and Ronald Herard. These photos, viewed as a group, gave the visitor a sense of Harlem, its good and bad neighborhoods, and its people. It was enlightening.

The Schomburg Center offers classes and lectures and is a pivotal heart of the neighborhood it serves.

The Skyscraper Museum

Location and Transit
39 Battery Place
(212) 968-1961
skyscraper.org
Subway: 1, 4, 5, R
Bus: M20

Hours and Admission

Wed.-Sun.	**12-6 p.m.**
Mon.-Tues.	**Closed**
Adults	**$5**
Seniors and students	**$2.50**

The Skyscraper Museum is an eye opener. In a relatively small space at the rear of the Ritz Carlton Hotel and Residence, it is located at the southern tip of Battery Park City among the original skyscrapers of the financial district and lower Manhattan. Walls, floors, and ceilings of the museum are a reflective, polished stainless steel, giving a visitor an immediate sensory experience of the museum's purpose, a celebration of the vertical steel and glass buildings of New York City and other cities worldwide.

One enters the gallery space on a steel ramp surrounded by a grey and white collage of cityscapes. Sunlight from large glass windows cause the ceiling and floor to glow. When we were there, the museum was showing *Future City 20/21,* a three-cycle exhibit that, in that moment, focused on a comparison of New York City and Shanghai. Google Earth Satellite maps of Manhattan and Shanghai covered two entire walls. They were big enough to identify individual streets and addresses.

Also featured in the museum were models of all kinds of impressive buildings, including the International Commerce Centre in Hong Kong, the fourth largest building in the world; the Shanghai World Financial Center, which looks like a giant bottle opener; the world's tallest building, the Burj Khalifa in Dubai; and the Shanghai Tower, a gently twisting triangle designed by Gensler Architects. Once completed, it will be the second largest building in the world.

The museum presents exhibitions that interpret skyscraper history and include development, design, construction, operation, and occupation of tall buildings all over the world. It displays architectural and engineering models, maps, blueprints, drawings, photographs, film, construction records, real estate surveys, and 3-D computer models. It provides visual and textual histories of skyscraper icons, such as the Empire State Building, the World Trade Center towers, and the Sears Tower in Chicago.

The museum also has a gift shop featuring products highlighting these architectural icons. The Skyscraper Museum serves as a wonderful introduction to the tall wonders of New York City and other structures around the world.

The Studio Museum in Harlem

Location and Transit

144 West 125th Street
(212) 864-4500
studiomuseum.org
Subway: 2, 3, 4, 5, 6, A, B, C, D
Bus: M2, M7, M10, M100, M101,
M102, BX15

Hours and Admission

Thurs.-Fri.	**12-9 p.m.**
Sat.	**10 a.m.-6 p.m.**
Sun.	**12-6 p.m.**
Mon.-Wed.	**Closed**
Adults	**$7**
Seniors and students with ID	**$3**
Members and children	
under 12	**Free**
Sun.	**Free**

Our trips up and down the borough of Manhattan exploring small museums have provided us with many surprises, not the least of which was the Studio Museum in Harlem. Tucked in among the bodegas, storefront churches, shops, and newsstands, this museum was an uplifting and totally engaging experience.

The Studio Museum in Harlem was founded in 1968 in a rented loft at 5th Avenue and 125th Street by community artists who were looking for welcoming studios where they could pursue their visions. From its inception, it also presented exhibitions and educational programs. Today, in a space donated by the New York Bank for Savings and magnificently renovated, it has not abandoned its original aims. While it is primarily an exhibition space for artists of African and Latino background, it also has an artist in residence program that gives three artists each year the extraordinary opportunity to pursue their work in well-equipped studios located on the third floor of the building.

In the expansive main-floor gallery, its vastness interrupted by white columns, we saw the work of Lynette Yiadom Boakye, a British painter of Ghanaian descent, who displayed very large portrait paintings, featuring people conjured only by the artist's imagination. In the enormous space, these enormous paintings were extraordinarily dramatic.

In *Alphabet*, Mark Bradford made use of found objects, including signs and posters, that reflect life in a local working-class community in South Los Angeles. These collages, which are scraped and then painted silver, pink, and blue, take the form of a complete alphabet. There were several more exhibits to see as well.

Our visit to the museum was topped off by a nice lunch in the museum's small café. We also spent a few pleasant minutes browsing the well-stocked gift shop.

Swiss Institute

Location and Transit
18 Wooster Street
(212) 925-2035
swissinstitute.net
Subway: 6, N, Q, R
Bus: M1, M6, M21

Hours and Admission

Wed.-Sun.	12-6 p.m.
Mon.-Tues.	Closed
Free	

The Swiss Institute was founded in 1986 and originally occupied two rooms at the Swiss Townhouse on West Sixty-Seventh Street. Since then, it has grown considerably and now makes its home in its own stand-alone building. The institute began as a showcase of Swiss art and artists, largely reaching a Swiss audience, but it has developed into a venue for contemporary art that provides a forum for cultural dialogue between Switzerland, Europe, and the United States.

We saw the work of the late Karlheinz Weinberger, a photographer with a focus on portraiture. Featured were black and white photographs of beautiful men, clothed and unclothed, taken in the 1950s and 60s for a gay underground club. For these photographs, referred to in the exhibit title as *The Intimate Stranger*, the artist used the pseudonym Jim Zurich. A second Weinberger exhibit, *Rebel Youth*, documented a portion of Swiss youth during the largely social rebellion of the 1960s. In addition to the photographs, glass cases featured denim jackets painted with all kinds of counter cultural designs. A curtained-off area showed a slide show of these people, who were rebelling against the conservative climate of the day.

The institute mounts a variety of exhibitions, both national and international, featuring artists from around the world.

The Tenement Museum

Location and Transit
103 Orchard Street
(212) 982-8420
tenement.org
Subway: B, D, F, J, M, Z
Bus: M15

Hours and Admission

Sun.-Sat.	**Guided tours only**
Adults	**$22**
Seniors and students	**$17**
Children under 6	**Not permitted**

The Tenement Museum makes available the history of a significant part of New York City's urban development—immigration and tenement apartment buildings. As we stood on a chilly Lower East Side Street across from the tenement we were about to visit, our guide explained that our explorations that day would show us how things change over time. It would also be a voyage of history made real.

Our small group entered 97 Orchard Street, a building built by Lukas Glockner, a German tailor, in 1863. We visited the tiny apartment of the Julius and Natalie Gumpertz family on the third floor, an apartment without electricity, bathrooms, or any of the modern conveniences we have all come to expect. Julius, a shoemaker, paid $10 a month for the apartment that was home to his family of four. Natalie's housekeeping difficulties came alive through descriptions of the many trips down to the backyard for water. He also described Julius's strange disappearance and Natalie's subsequent strength earning a living for herself and her daughters. The Gumpertz family was among the original influx of German and Irish immigrants to the Lower East Side, their first home in the United States.

When the Germans began moving out of the Lower East Side in the 1890s, the Eastern Europeans and Italian immigrants moved in. The Tenement Museum also has reconstructed the family home of the

Baldizzis, who occupied an apartment at 97 Orchard Street beginning in 1928. By comparison to the Gompertz family, this Italian family's life was much easier, as it is described by the daughter of the family in a wonderful recording. The kitchen had a sink and an ice box. A gas heater on the wall, fed by coins, heated the water.

The building at 97 Orchard Street that has echoes of so many new Americans lay empty from 1935 until it was acquired by the museum in 1992. The 1935 building law required fire-proofing, and the then-landlord, who could not afford to do so, turned his tenants out and closed the building.

The Tenement Museum is expanding to another site which will outline the lives of Hispanics and Asians, more recent immigrants to the Lower East Side. The Visitor Center has bathrooms and computer programs featuring the highlights of the museum. The reconstructed tenement building has no bathrooms or air conditioning and is not wheelchair accessible. The museum offers a variety of one-hour tours of different apartments and social situations.

Photograph by Keiko Nl

Photograph by Keiko Nl

Theodore Roosevelt Birthplace

Location and Transit
28 East 20th Street
(212) 260-1616
nps.gov/thrb
Subway: 4, 5, 6, L, R
Bus: M1, M2, M3, M5, M23

Hours and Admission
Tues.-Sat.	**9 a.m.-5 p.m.**
Sun.-Mon.	**Closed**

Guided tours for period rooms only,
   on the hour every hour except
   12 p.m.
Free

Theodore Roosevelt was the only president born in New York City, and the home where he lived until he was eight years old is open to the public. His former home is a completely restored brownstone that gives visitors a glimpse into the early life of our twenty-sixth president and his family. It also gives us a good idea of how comfortably New Yorkers might have lived during the late nineteenth century.

The home is part of the United States National Park system, and it constitutes two side-by-side brownstones dating from 1848. One, which had been owned by Theodore's father, is the house as it existed in Theodore's youth. The other, formerly owned by Theodore's uncle, houses a museum devoted to artifacts that chronicle Roosevelt's life as a child, adult, politician, hunter, and roughrider. Here, one can see Theodore's white, intricately embroidered christening outfit as well as the shirt, replete with bullet hole, that he wore when he was shot in an attempted assassination. There are family pictures galore, animal skins testifying to his skill as a hunter, newspaper clippings, and scores of books that he authored. The birthplace has a small elevator installed by Theodore's sister, Anna, who was disabled.

We visited the library, which Theodore called the gloomiest room in the house. The room had no windows of its own and was lit by flickering gas lamps, so indeed, the young Roosevelt was probably correct. The books lining the room are all from the Roosevelt family collection.

The knowledgeable ranger who showed us around informed us that 70 percent of the artifacts were original to the house. The other 30 percent were exact copies of those that had been used by the Roosevelt family. The wallpapers throughout the house were printed from actual templates of the original wallpapers. Wall-to-wall floor coverings were made from the designs of the original oval rugs covering most of the floors in the house.

Theodore's bedroom was next to the back porch, on which his father had placed gymnasium equipment to strengthen the puny, asthma afflicted little boy. We also saw the master bedroom and the double bed where Theodore was born.

There is a small shop that stocks books about Theodore Roosevelt and his times.

Tibet House US

Location and Transit

22 West 15th Street
(212) 807-0563
tibethouse.us
Subway: 1, 2, 3, 4, 5, 6, 9, F, L, R
Bus: M1, M2, M3, M4, M5, M6

Hours and Admission

Mon.-Fri.	11 a.m.-6 p.m.
Sun.	11 a.m.-4 p.m.
Sat.	Closed
Free	

If you were to look through the Tibet House magazine, *Drum*, you may see some familiar names: scholar Robert A. F. Thurman; Uma Thurman; Philip Glass, the composer who also is vice president of the organization; and Patti Smith are all involved in the organization. Even without exploring Tibetan Buddhism, Tibet House savors the art of this extraordinary culture.

Tibet House is dedicated to preserving Tibet's unique culture at a time when that small country is confronted with possible extinction on its own soil. It is part of a worldwide network of Tibetan institutions committed to ensuring that Tibetan culture never disappears. Tibet House was established in the United States in 1987 at the request of the Dalai Lama. Much of the art and the extensive library in Tibet House are part of the Repatriation Collection, held in safekeeping and meant to be returned to the Tibetan people when it is appropriate for its safety. The library is available for quiet study.

When we visited, the formal gallery exhibition took our breath away. Here was a large room full of exquisite tangka paintings. The exhibit was named *The Menris Tradition of Tibetan Tangka Art: Traditional Paintings by the New Generation in Exile.* The beautiful, intricately designed paintings we saw were not old but recently created by students at the Institute of Tibetan Thangka Art in Dharamsala, India. The Menris tradition is characterized by clear outlines, strong colors, fine shadings, and golden accents. Guided tours and an information sheet outlining the complex symbols are available to visitors, if desired.

Also in the gallery as a permanent fixture is the Lhakang Shrine, created by Tibetan artists and accessible to the public.

Tibet House has a little jewel of a gift shop and offers lectures and classes to the general public at a moderate cost. It does not have an eating facility, but the downtown neighborhood offers many places for food.

The Ukrainian Museum

Location and Transit

222 East 6th Street
(212) 228-0110
ukrainianmuseum.org
Subway: 6, F, N, R
Bus: M1, M2, M3, M8, M15,
M101, M102, M103

Hours and Admission

Wed.-Sun.	**11:30 a.m.-5 p.m.**	
Mon.-Tues.		**Closed**
Adults		**$8**
Seniors and students with ID		**$6**
Members and children		
under 12		**Free**

On the Lower East Side, surrounded by the buildings that once were part of a vibrant Ukrainian neighborhood, stands the structure of the Ukrainian Museum, erected in 2005. It is an important resource for the existing community, which includes St. George Ukrainian Catholic Church and rectory, the Ukrainian Baptist Church, the Ukrainian Sports Club, the Ukrainian Center, and several Ukrainian restaurants, all in a radius of several blocks.

This small jewel of a museum was founded in 1976 by the Ukrainian National Women's League of America and has always been committed to the preservation and propagation of Ukrainian art and culture. The museum produces exhibitions, scholarships, educational programs, publications, and community events.

The museum holds one of the most important Ukrainian folk art collections outside of Ukraine. We saw brightly colored wedding and festive clothing, ritual cloths, kilim weavings, and other beautifully embroidered and woven textiles from various areas of Ukraine. We loved the richly decorated, brilliantly colored designs of Easter eggs, for which Ukraine is rightly famous. In addition, the museum holds collections of beautiful ceramics, metalwork, brass and silver jewelry, and carved wooden objects.

We enjoyed looking at the fine arts collections, which included paintings, drawings, graphic works, and sculpture created by Ukrainian artists across the globe. This museum's rich holdings provided us with an elementary grounding in the art and artists of Ukraine, including Nikifor, Vasyl Krychevsky, Alexander Archipenko, Oleksa Novakivsky, and Lev Getz.

When we were there, the museum was showing one of its many special exhibits featuring the wonderful paintings of Arcadia Olenska-Petryshyn. This exhibit was compiled from gifts to the museum of forty-four paintings from Olenska-Petryshyn's husband, Dr. Wolodymyr Petryshyn, four from her mother, and other pieces given by collectors. Her work ran the gamut from early paintings of objective reality to wildly colored abstract expressionist canvases to lovely nature paintings evocative of Ukrainian primitivism.